YoungWriters 200

PLAYGRO

Let your creativity flow...

ode

limerick   haiku

rhyme

ball...

- Baby Bards Vol II
Edited by Steve Twelvetree

 Young**Writers**

First published in Great Britain in 2006 by:
Young Writers
Remus House
Coltsfoot Drive
Peterborough
PE2 9JX
Telephone: 01733 890066
Website: www.youngwriters.co.uk

SB ISBN 1 84602 393 9

Foreword

Young Writers was established in 1991 and has been passionately devoted to the promotion of reading and writing in children and young adults ever since. The quest continues today. Young Writers remains as committed to the fostering of burgeoning poetic and literary talent as ever.

This year's Young Writers competition has proven as vibrant and dynamic as ever and we are delighted to present a showcase of the best poetry from across the UK. Each poem has been carefully selected from a wealth of *Playground Poets* entries before ultimately being published in this, our thirteenth primary school poetry series.

Once again, we have been supremely impressed by the overall high quality of the entries we have received. The imagination, energy and creativity which has gone into each young writer's entry made choosing the best poems a challenging and often difficult but ultimately hugely rewarding task - the general high standard of the work submitted amply vindicating this opportunity to bring their poetry to a larger appreciative audience.

We sincerely hope you are pleased with our final selection and that you will enjoy *Playground Poets - Baby Bards Vol II* for many years to come.

Contents

Beaconhill Community First School, Cramlington

Brandon Beat (7)	16
Aimee Nelson (7)	17
Lewis Younger (8)	17
Katrina Ouzman (8)	18
Olivia Sarginson (7)	18
Liam Richardson (7)	19
Bethany Sanderson (7)	19
Kayleigh Jewitt (7)	19
Carl Parry (8)	20
Ronan S Jennings (7)	20
Sean Lazonby (7)	21
Shannon English (8)	21
John Wilkinson (8)	22
Brent Richardson (8)	22
Caitlin McMillan (7)	22
Connor Jackson (7)	23
Ellie Millar (7)	23
Jaimie Davison-Stewart (7)	23
Josh White (8)	24
Dylan Darbyshire	24
Mathew Davidson (7)	25
Ki Green (7)	25
Courtney Thompson (7)	25
John Abbott (7)	26
Nikita Stephenson (7)	26
Jack Hindle (8)	26
Joseph Luke (8)	27
Charlotte Perry (8)	28
Laurie Bramwell (8)	29
Courtney Egerton (8)	30
Callum Nelson (8)	31
Abbie Paxton (7)	32
Shannon Fantozzi (8)	33
Courtney Lamb (8)	34
Thomas Jewitt (8)	35
George Tweddell Brown (8)	36
Cameron Scott (7)	37
Siobhan Wilkinson (9)	38
Ashleigh Beat (8)	39

Demi-Lee Marshall (7)   40
Sarah-Louise Young (7)   40

Bromham CE Lower School, Bromham
Katie Webb (7)   41
Jordan Warwick (7)   41
Chloe Preston (8)   42
Marley Newland (7)   42
Emma Patrickson (8)   43
Megan Wallace (7)   43
James Gillum (8)   44
James Thomson (7)   44
Joe Tebbett (8)   45
Ben Hammond (7)   45
Nathan Weightman (7)   46
James Harding (8)   46
Thomas O'Neill (7)   46

Carmountside Primary School, Stoke-on-Trent
Thomas Whitby (9)   47
Jake Britchfield (9)   47
Bradley Hancock (8)   48
James Wright (8)   48
Samuel Thurston (8)   49
Julia Unwin (9)   49
Kieron Thompson (8)   50
Bradley Stevenson (9)   50
Tonicha Brett (9)   51
Hollie Munday (8)   51
Rebecca Matthews (8)   52
Reegan Harvey (8)   52
Molly Newton (8)   53
Christian Longshaw (8)   53
Sharna Baskerville (8)   54

Cumbernauld Primary School, Cumbernauld
Scott Shaw (11)   54
Fiona Dalling (10)   55
Kara Graham (10)   55
Fraser Doyle (10)   55
Olivia Roxburgh-Begg (10)   56

Laura Campbell (10)   56
Andrew Norman (10)   56
Jordan Maclean (10)   57
Rebecca Blair (10)   57
Paige Mitchelson (10)   58
Samantha Davidson (10)   58
Hannah Johnstone (10)   59
Cara Dalziel (10)   59
Olivia Bryant (10)   60
Ryan Dukes (10)   60
Sophie Thomson (10)   60
Amy Sutherland (10)   61
Kayleigh Standish (10)   61
Claudia Smith (10)   62
Ben Chok (9)   62
Kerrie Campbell (10)   63
Nadia Wilson (10)   63
Amanda Valentine (10)   64
Stephanie Minnes (9)   64

Elworth Hall Primary School, Sandbach
Matthew Frost (9)   65
Thomas Wilson (10)   65
Sarah Evans (9)   66
Daniel Powell (9)   66
Rachel Shufflebotham (9)   67
Frankie Potter (9)   67
Chris Stroud (10)   68
Oliver Thompson (9)   68

Garswood Primary School, Garswood
Jasmine Harland (9)   69
Chloe Ratcliffe-Cross (9)   69
Francesca Miller (9)   69
Amy Baker (9)   70
Heather Chadwick (8)   70
Matthew Nolan (9)   71
Sophie Spanner (8)   71
Jake Blackburn   71
Megan Seaman (11)   72
Sophie Atherton (9)   72

Joe Donovan (11)   73
Lucy Robinson (11)   73
Caitlin Hewitt (11)   74
Amy Reeves (9)   74
Laura Fletcher   75
Elicia-May Donlevy (9)   75
Liam Fazakerley (9)   75
Lucy Rimmer (9)   76
Jack Savage (9)   76
Rachael Green (9)   76
Rebecca Adamson   77
Callum Goundry (9)   77
Gareth Jones (9)   77
Joshua Mather (9)   78
Megan Walsh (9)   78
Lauren Brown (10)   78
Charlotte Wiswell (11)   79
Jade Hough (10)   79
Victoria Hateley (10)   79
Collette Topping (11)   80
Matthew Porter (10)   80
Ashleigh Latham (10)   81
Mark Randall (10)   81
Jake Hamilton (10)   82
Chelsey Thompson (10)   82
Lauren Austin (10)   82
Bethany Fairhurst (10)   83
Abbie Larkin (11)   83
Ashley Smith (10)   84
Lucy Carter (10)   84
Rachel Burgess (10)   85

Gorran Primary School, Coleraine

Hannah Kennedy (9)   85
Oliver Jamieson (10)   86
Richard Clyde (9)   86
Hannah Gault (8)   86
Rachel Kelly (8)   87
Shane Donnelly (10)   87
Jamie Boreland (10)   88
Peter Linton (9)   88

Jordan Neely (9)   88
Shanden McDowell (10)   89
Timothy McNeill (9)   89
Nicole Boreland (8)   90
Emma Moore (9)   90
Annabel Steen (8)   91
Zoe Gibson (9)   91
Jordan Gregg (8)   92

Haydock English Martyrs RC Primary School, Haydock
Charlotte Smith (10)   92
Jamie Harrison (10)   93
Adam Forshaw (9)   93
Charlotte Hull (10)   94
Luke Pilkington (10)   94
Callum Jackson (10)   94
Lauren Mason (10)   95
Rece Whitfield ((9)   95
Chelsea Smith (10)   96
Alex Harrison (9)   96
Lana Kayattiankal (10)   97
Thomas Kilgannon (10)   97
Katie Woodward (10)   98
Katie Edwards (10)   98
Jack Day (9)   99
Chloe Dowd (10)   99
Jacob Adair (10)   100
Connor Hewitt (10)   100

Hillbourne Middle School, Poole
Sophie Allisett (11)   101
Katie Sneddon (9)   102
Charlie Jones (9)   102
Sarah Benfield (11)   103
Charlie Bishop (8)   103
Aimee Auger (10)   104
Christine Lovell (10)   104
Ella Brooks (10)   105

Holystone Primary School, Newcastle upon Tyne

Jessica Wiffin (10)   105
Alice Higgins (11)   106
Brooke Foster (10)   106
Juliette Amers (10)   107
Rosie Duerdin (10)   107
Kayleigh Leung (9)   108
Lauren Scollins (10)   108

Horsenden Primary School, Greenford

Cherelle Whyte (9)   109
Yasir Khan   109
Ritu Elaswarapu (9)   110
Saawan Parekh (9)   110
Shehan Dasan (9)   111
Jemma Laird (9)   112
Elizabeth Appleby (9)   113
Dushan Despotovic (9)   114
Bhavethaa Barathithasan (10)   114
Anuthya Nambirajah (9)   115
Aneesha Bhumber (10)   116
Bethany Marshall (9)   116
Edward Nana-Ansah   117
Rianne Shiebak   117
Charlene De Alwis (9)   118
Vinay Vaghijani (9)   118
Christian Gonzalez (9)   119
Shabri Mehta (9)   119
Anitta Sritharan (9)   120
Tharsika Muralitharan (10)   120
Louisa Stivaros (10)   121
Fatema Sulemanji (10)   121
Laura Youna (10)   122
Mona Jamil (10)   123
Avinash Bakshi (9)   124
Radhika Bathia (9)   124
Aaron Eni   125
Sharihaan Ahmad (9)   125
Sumiyya Iqbal (9)   126
Hana Jali (9)   126
Angela Lam (10)   127

Kush Bhandari (9)	128
Tayyaba Ahmad (9)	129
Luke Campbell (9)	130
Khaled Abdellatiff (9)	130
Maryam Bux (9)	131
Chloe Charles (9)	131
Neeki Doroudian (9)	132
Nidhi Sunderam (10)	133
Roshni Rabheru (9)	134
Zoya Hussain (10)	134
Stephen Danes (9)	135
Dina Morsy-Fahmy (9)	135
James Walton (9)	136
Laylan Siddik (9)	137
Dean Boothe (9)	137
Hashim Hussain (9)	138
Sara Tofiq (9)	138
Daniel Cox (9)	139
Naim Rahim	140

Lammack Primary School, Blackburn

Maariyah Esat (11)	140
Charlotte Jackson (10)	141
Thomas Johnson (10)	141
Zahra Bahadur (11)	142
Ayesha Ougradar (11)	142
Mehreen Shah (11)	142
Heather Mashiter (10)	143
Aamirah Hasan (10)	143
Linzi Robertson (10)	143
Grace Handscomb (10)	144
Kasongo Swana (10)	144
Amelia Dunning (10)	145
Fern Nicholas (11)	145
Sophie Jones (10)	146
Yusuf Dardouri (10)	146
Daniel Webster (10)	146
Matthew Ebbs (10)	147
Alia Malik	147
Ayaz Patel (10)	147
Humaira Musa (11)	148

Hennah Patel (10)   148
Sadeya Abhujl (11)   149

Lees Hill Primary School, Brampton
Maisie Nicholson (9)   149
Alice Hudson (10)   150
Rachel Riddle (8)   150
Isobel Mortimer (10)   151
Arran Forster   152

Lightcliffe Preparatory School
Benjamin Armitage (9)   152
Thomas Lathom-Sharp (9)   153
Thomas Richardson (9)   153
Liam Stedman (9)   154
Rachael Currie (9)   154
Rebecca Firth (10)   155
Ellie Sloane (9)   155
Emma Shooter (9)   156
Olivia Wright (9)   156
Beth Burnhill (9)   157
Cameron Wroot (9)   157
Lucy Sheard (10)   158
Abbygail Robertshaw (9)   158
Hean Yeung-Lee (9)   159
Emma Leonard (10)   159
Danielle North (9)   160
Oliver Firth (10)   160

Linlithgow Bridge Primary School, Linlithgow
Ross MacLeod (9)   161
Jensen Gardner (9)   161
Ben Milne (9)   162
Madeleine Nicholls (9)   163
Eilidh Stewart (9)   164
Hannah McMonagle Johnston (8)   165
Hannah Johnston (9)   166
Catherine Wilson (9)   166
Catriona Charlton (9)   167
Catherine Tuckett (9)   167
Kate Harrower (9)   168

Alison Tulloch (9)   169
Gemma Samson (9)   170
Andrew MacDonald (9)   171
Michael Currie (9)   172
Ardal Miller (9)   173
Joanna Boxall (9)   174
Daniel Beaton (9)   175
Ross Cruickshanks (9)   176
Harriet Reeder (9)   177
Barbara Hogan (9)   178
Cameron Atkinson (9)   179
Alice Newey (9)   180
Daniel Nimmo (9)   181

Lyndon Preparatory School, Colwyn Bay
Elizabeth Richards (8)   181

Melbourne Park Primary School, Chelmsford
Lorna Dunn (10)   182
Erin Parkhurst (8)   182
Abigail Loble (10)   183
Keeleigh Hammond (8)   183
Jamie Ripton (10)   184
Alexander Sullivan (9)   184
Bradley Mardell (10)   185
Billy Buckingham (11)   185
Anthony Reval (10)   186
Josh Cormack-Butler (9)   186
Ashley Gorham (7)   186
Kaylem Skitch (9)   187
Lachlan Stanley (7)   187
Daniel Potter   187
Kaycee O'Sullivan (8)   188
Katy Edwards (7)   188
Kurtis Mclaren (8)   188
Charley Gorham (9)   189
Jack Muir (9)   189
Daniel Ripton (8)   189
Melissa Eden (8)   190
Mercedes Babij (10)   190
Kelli-Ann Chapman (7)   190

James Carter (8)	191
Ryan Moore (9)	191
Liam Brown (9)	191
Tommy Silvey (8)	192
Jessica Little (7)	192
Lauren-Ann Hart (8)	192
Levi-Wayne Stanley (9)	193
Andrew Pearce (10)	193
Jennifer Clark (10)	194
Steven Drew (10)	194
Emma Hope (8)	194
Ashman Elles (8)	195
Kiera Cagney (8)	195
Laura Theedom (9)	196
Tanya Jervis (7)	196
Courtney Clarke (8)	197
Nigel Stratford (9)	197
Shannon Grinstead (8)	197
Ashley Byford (8)	198
Daniel Coleman (7)	198
Luke Brown (7)	198

Oaklands Primary School, Welwyn

Hannah Ford (10)	199
Philippa Stephens (7)	199
Katherine Woods (10)	200
Laura Goodacre (7)	200
Hannah Kempster (9)	201
Zara Hoy (7)	201
Katie Genever (7)	202
Robert Drew (7)	202
Ben Wilson (7)	202
Robert White (8)	203
William Vaughan (7)	203
Adam Webster (7)	204
Katie Deards (7)	204
Alastair Drew (7)	204
Connor Wilson (9)	205
Bethany Kendle (8)	205
Cara Beard (8)	206
Jamie Kempster (8)	206

Vishva Naik (8)	206
Jessica Hall (7)	207
Daniel Rice (8)	207
Jade Taylor (7)	207
Rhys Carter-Atkinson (10)	208
Oliver Mawer (7)	208
George Wallis-Smith (8)	209
Rachael Writer-Davies (10)	209
Hannah Young (8)	210
Erin Van-Tam (7)	210
Emily Tomlinson (8)	211
Sian Fuller (7)	211
Ged Wren (10)	212
Heather Holden (7)	212
Robert Vaughan (9)	213
Ryan O'Driscoll (9)	213
Oliver Stephens (9)	214
Adam Nye (11)	214
Joshua Heyman (9)	215
Maxwell Brendish (8)	215
Brodie Collingwood (9)	216
Thomas Deards (10)	216
Louise Graham (9)	217
Mark Wong (9)	217
Callum France (10)	218
Josh Genever (10)	218
Alexander Woods (9)	218
Bryony Smith (9)	219
Ellis Blake (8)	219
Simon Goldsmith (9)	220
Samuel Borrie (9)	220
Rhian Mather (9)	221
Luke Fuller (9)	221
Matthew Catterick (11)	222
Harvey Turner (8)	222
Richard Vaughan (9)	223
Georgina Shortland (9)	223
Adam Wetherall (9)	224
George Ironton (10)	224
Emily Beswick (9)	225
Joel Khalili (10)	225
Charlotte Birtles (8)	226

The Poems

Seasons On The Earth

Spring is the first season of the year
New buds are coming with a smile
Happy birds are singing on the trees
New life and new things are here

Summer is the second season of the year
Lots of sun shining and very hot
Children are at the seaside
New plants and coloured flowers are everywhere

Autumn is the third season of the year
Cold, windy weather make leaves fall
From the trees here and there
Leaves, leaves everywhere

Winter is the last season of the year
The coldest, freezing frost and black ice
Dry fruits and hot, hot chocolate
White, white snow and lots of fun
Holidays and Christmas here
Merry Christmas!

Safa Azra Saeed (10)

Tree

As tall as a misty mountain covered in snow,
As wide as a car shining in the sun,
As rough as a crocodile's scales on a summer day,
As smooth as a poppy petal,
As colourful as a swallow curving in the sky,
As still as a yellow, shining lion just about to pounce,
Yet, as twirly as a spiral staircase shining in the sun,
As bright as a crystal glistening in the moonlight,
Yet, as gloomy as a dark room with bats flying around
                                                a lightless ceiling,
But above all, as beautiful as a jay flying around the wood.

Henry Seymour (8)

Trees

As tall as a slippery skyscraper,
As wide as a misty, mysterious mountain,
As rough as rocky slabs,
Yet, as smooth as a slithery snake,
As colourful as a ragged rainbow,
As beautiful as a butterfly, browsing in the breeze,
Yet, as busy as a bee, buzzing.
As boisterous as a buffalo, bellowing in the sand,
But, above all, as beautiful as a rainbow.

Robert Turner (8)

All About Colours

Green is the colour of the nice, fresh grass
Orange is the colour of Irn Bru in my glass
Blue is the colour of the nice, blue sky
Black is the colour of a black eye
Purple is the colour of my lipgloss
Pink is the colour of candyfloss
Yellow is my brother's favourite colour
Red is the colour of loving one another.

Monica Watt (9)

Trees

As tall as a flaming volcano,
As wide as a remarkable mountain, covered in snow,
As jagged as a sharp hedgehog,
Yet, as smooth as moon glow.
As colourful as a charming butterfly,
As grand as the boiling hot sun,
As soft as rain falling from a silky, grey sky,
Yet, above all, as beautiful as a smiley flower.

James Milhench (8)

Trees

As high as a flaming volcano that is erupting,
As wide as a massive, freezing ice cube,
As rough as a charging elephant,
Yet, as smooth as a thick, fat, moving log,
As colourful as a sparkling rainbow, blazing in the sunlight,
But, above all, as beautiful as a stunning sunflower.

Gavin Wilton (8)

Trees

As tall as a skyscraper sitting sparkling in the sun,
As wide as an elephant lying down,
As rough as a piece of sandpaper smoothing out some wood,
Yet, as smooth as a pebble sitting on a beach,
As colourful as a rainbow between two clouds,
As soft as a stripy scarf wrapped around someone's neck,
Yet, as spiky as a needle pricking a finger,
As elegant as a ballet dancer dancing on a stage,
But, above all, as beautiful as a butterfly fluttering around.

Hannah Cocking (10)

Trees

As tall as a flaming volcano,
As wide as a thick, fat log,
As rough as a piece of dark bark,
Yet, as smooth as brown chocolate, waiting to be eaten.
As colourful as a glistening work of art,
As brown as a fat, smooth conker,
Yet, above all, as beautiful as a swaying kite.

Laura Saxby (8)

Whenever

Whenever the sun has gone,
Whenever the wind is gusty
And the trees are howling for help,
A man is galloping over the crunchy leaves.
The creatures hide in the dark, gloomy bushes,
As the noise of the hooves rattles in their ears.

Harry Notman (9)

Whenever

Whenever the squirrel is cracking a nut,
Whenever the leaves are crunching,
While the toads leap in the water,
A mysterious girl is dancing,
Her skirt twirling, her hair twirling,
It's a marvellous place to be.

Whenever the vole scurries along,
Whenever the badger scurries out of his set,
While the fox catches his prey,
The mysterious girl is dancing,
Her skirt swirling, her hair twirling,
It's a marvellous place to be.

Edina Morris (10)

Whenever

Whenever the sky is grey,
Whenever the sky is full of clouds,
There will be a hound, brown and white,
Hunting a fox.
As the hound sniffs out the fox's den,
The hunters shoot them.

John Sheppard (8)

Trees

As tall as a marvellous, purple-headed mountain,
As wide as a shining silver bus, rolling down the street,
As rough as a wall, not painted white,
Yet, as smooth as a pink poppy petal,
As colourful as a remarkable rainbow,
As brown as a creepy, crunchy leaf,
As still as an owl,
Yet, as gloomy as a dark, frightful street,
Yet, above all, as beautiful as a rainbow trout in a river.

Chloe Felton (8)

Haiku

In the spooky wood
Lies a cute, prickly hedgehog
Curled up in a ball.

Toni Wilton (10)

Trees

As tall as a skyscraper in the sun,
As wide as a sandy desert,
As rough as cardboard,
Yet, as smooth as a newborn baby's skin.
As colourful as autumn leaves falling from the tree,
As elegant as a ballet dancer,
Yet, as dazzling as a firework,
As gigantic as an elephant,
But, above all, as beautiful as a flower in the breeze.

Becky Pearson (9)

Trees

As tall as a volcano filled with crimson lava,
As wide as an immense library,
As rough as an uneven path,
Yet, as smooth as a new white sheet of paper,
As colourful as a sleek rainbow,
As cared for as a loved dog,
As pretty as the shining dew,
Yet, as brown as a conker,
As solid as a brick,
With leaves as crunchy as a cracker,
As curvy as ivy climbing up a wall,
But, above all, as beautiful as a flower, shining in the sunlight.

Katie Little (8)

Whenever

Whenever the wind is howling,
Whenever the night falls,
All night long, in the damp, drizzly darkness,
A man walks the streets at night,
Late at night, when the lights are out.
Why does he walk about?

Whenever the boats are tossed about at sea
And all children are in bed,
When the streets are covered in snow
And the road is covered in ice,
The man walks at night,
Never in the daylight.

Harvey Bridge-Edwards (9)

Tree

As tall as a chimney puffing out its smoke into the scarlet sky,
As wide as waves in a pool of water, hitting rocks on a sandy shore,
As rough as a pavement getting trampled on,
Yet, as smooth as a grain of sand, dropping into the spider's web,
before the spider comes.
As colourful as a rainbow, disappearing in the sky,
As marvellous as melted chocolate dripping into a mouth,
Yet, as curvy as a pig's tail wagging in the mud.
But, above all, as beautiful as a flower bed with bees around.

Sophie Coles (9)

Sky Surfer

Sky-surfing through the night
I gave the neighbours such a fright
Wind dancing past your window
I knock over Mrs McWindow

After my great venture through the street
Two clouds do they meet
They send down such a watery splash
To get out of the rain I must dash!

Knocking me down out of the sky
I can't even tell my owner goodbye
I'm sent spinning through the air
This sends my owner into right despair

After my expedition towards the moon
I will get home very, very soon.

Scott Hilditch (10)
Ashby CE Primary School, Ashby-De-La-Zouch

Agile Flyer

I swiftly move,
Across the sky,
I'm very agile,
You may not know why.

Red in colour,
Yellow and green tail,
I fly high in the air,
Without fail.

Cars and buses,
I see down low,
I don't know why,
They go so slow.

Moving left,
Moving right,
The reason is -
I am a kite!

Megan Booth (11)
Ashby CE Primary School, Ashby-De-La-Zouch

Conquerer

I swoop and slide around the sky,
Being a sky-turner and a dazzling twizzler.
I soar to and fro in the day
And free as an eagle in the eye-catching night.
Roaming the sky, gracefully I dive around,
People call me a wind stalker as I glide.

I'm colourful and bright, it's hard to miss me,
As I ride the wind like a jockey on a horse.
I emerge from behind clouds
And I twist round trees.

I am an air-conquering heart-stopper.

Alexandra Blackburn (10)
Ashby CE Primary School, Ashby-De-La-Zouch

My Kite

My kite is normal,
It is yellow with blue spots.
My kite waves to me when it's up in the air.
It is free and exciting,
It dips and dives.

My kite dances in the wind,
Soaring to and fro.
My kite is special,
When it goes up and down,
With help and glee.

My kite is special and fun,
I would run with it all day.
It is special and beautiful.
I like my kite and my mum likes it too,
It is fun and it is my own.

Amy Spicer (10)
Ashby CE Primary School, Ashby-De-La-Zouch

Kite Festival

Kites all free and eye-catching,
Thin kites, fat kites and colourful square kites,
Circular kites and ones like you,
Ones like buses, trains and cars too,
Kites, kites, do you like kites?

Rapidly racing through the air,
Crashing and darting everywhere,
Dancing in the wind, up and down,
Kites, kites, do you like kites?

Jamie Eydman (11)
Ashby CE Primary School, Ashby-De-La-Zouch

Kite

Up and down through the air,
Going through like no one cares.

In the shape of a great big ball,
Going up and up till it's really tall.

Up and down through the air,
Going through like no one cares.

Going round with a silly face,
Challenging anyone to a race.

Up and down through the air,
Going through like no one cares.

Soaring through the bright, bright night,
This is the most amazing kite.

Up and down through the air,
Going through like no one cares.

Helen Starkey (11)
Ashby CE Primary School, Ashby-De-La-Zouch

A Kite's Flight

A kite's flight is high and mighty,
It soars through the air looking for breaks in the wind,
With its long, silky, valiant tail after it.
Swooping, twirling and whirling freely,
It gracefully glides through all terrain.

This magnificent kite finely stitched is astonishing,
Coated with a beautiful golden-brown touch.

Benedict Berrow (10)
Ashby CE Primary School, Ashby-De-La-Zouch

The Kite And I Having Fun!

I swirl so gently in the sky,
Trying not to fly so high,
I use my colours to attract people I see,
Swooping to and fro, making me glide over the sea!

I am a red circle with a dragon inside,
Waiting for someone to witness me,
Jumping and twirling,
Imaginative and amazing,
I am so proud to be!

Astonishing is me,
Waiting to be let free,
I will be a heart-stopper,
Then turn into a wind-rider,
That is me!

What it is to be a kite,
Jumping and diving through the sea, waiting for another flight,
I am always happy wherever I go,
I will never turn around and refuse, that's so,
That's the reason you should use me!

I can be used in all weather,
And now you know my special power,
Now you know what I can do,
You can fly me through the snow,
So come on, let's be friends!

Abigail Tracey (10)
Ashby CE Primary School, Ashby-De-La-Zouch

Why Are You A Kite?

Why are you so agile
Like a bird that never lands?
Your pattern's so imaginative
Like a dozen waving hands.

Why do you sway to and fro
In the gentle breathing air?
I'd always like that, up on clouds
Floating without a care.

Why are you a ballet dancer
The blue sky as your floor?
Dipping, diving, swerving, gliding
Like you were once four.

Why do you like conquering Earth
Flying as if it's yours?
Maybe you're a Viking boat
Without any oars.

But when you've had enough up there
You see that bright green turf,
Stalling swiftly, falling quickly
Spiralling down to Earth.

Naomi Edwards (11)
Ashby CE Primary School, Ashby-De-La-Zouch

Wind-Rider

Kite black
Kite blue
Kite fair
Kite dashing through the air.

Kite turn
Kite burn
Kite glide
Kite glide with pride.

Kite dive
Kite strive
Kite speed
Kite coming with my need.

Kite fly
Kite sky
Kite spin
Kite with a nose like a pin.

Kite stall
Kite fall
Kite glider
I am the wind-rider.

Liam Johnson (10)
Ashby CE Primary School, Ashby-De-La-Zouch

Raise The Dead

Round about the cauldron go,
In our ingredients we will throw,

To make our spell we shall raise hell,
To wake the dead with our yell,

Our cauldron is ready for the taking,
Our spell is in the making,

Deadly nightshade, put it in,
Eye of newt and human skin,

Whale's fin, gall of tiger,
Dragon's ear and bone of spider,

Cauldron of a poisoned gorilla,
And the chest of his killer,

A phoenix wing and crocodile's toes,
A horse's head and dead man's nose,

A scorpion's sting, dead shark's liver,
This spell will make you shiver,

Black widow's head will raise the dead,
Come all spirits be by us led,

Double, double, toil and trouble,
Make our cauldron heat and bubble!

Jamie Keane (10)
Bader Primary School, Stockton-on-Tees

Dancing Flames

I saw the flames playing and leaping,
Spitting ashes at children sleeping,
The dog of fire ran through the wood,
Spinning and turning, destroying the good,
Crackling and hissing, the fire breathes out,
Killing the people, making them shout.

Kieran Davies (11)
Bader Primary School, Stockton-on-Tees

A Spell To Turn Teachers Into Germs

Round about the cauldron fly,
Point thou cauldron to the sky,
For we added the things we could,
To make the charm thick and good.

Eye of fish, claw of bird,
Bloody guts of sleeping herd,
Lightning bolts and paw of hound,
These are some of the things we found.

Beaks of swan, a baby's cry,
Nose of dog, horse's thigh,
Tail of newt, gut of bee,
The broken shell of a long-dead flea.

Liver-filled shell, bucket of blood,
Fly's wing and lice-filled wood,
Fillet of worm, eye of hound,
Herbs and spices by the pound.

Abbie Pasco (11)
Bader Primary School, Stockton-on-Tees

To Turn All Teachers Into Slime-Covered Toads

Round about the cauldron go,
Into the pot our charms we'll throw,
I'll throw thou in first of all
And poisoned snake, slim and tall,
Troll's eye second, bee's sting third,
Beak of singing blue tit bird,
Next we'll throw in a few more things,
Tail of cat for whom night-time sings,
Hag's warty nose aged for a hundred years,
Claws of two polar bears,
Werewolf's blood comes in next,
Moon's eclipse and a tramp's yellow fingertips.

Bethany Fleming (10)
Bader Primary School, Stockton-on-Tees

A Spell

Round about the cauldron go,
In the poisoned entrails throw,
Tarantula's legs and scorpion's sting,
Tongue of dog and eye of bush baby,
Poisoned entrails of a frog,
Then the venom of a troll,
Round about the cauldron go,
Fire burn and cauldron bubble,
Toe of Turk and powdered brain,
Witch's wart and porcupine's quills,
Eye of newt and sting of bee,
Snout of hog and dragonfly's wing,
Round about the cauldron go,
Fire burn and cauldron bubble.

Andrew Hill (10)
Bader Primary School, Stockton-on-Tees

Kennings Poem

Heat maker
Steam riser
Sweat dripper
Skin burner
Eye dazzler
Temperature riser
Water heater
Body warmer
Body sweater
House heater
Floor breaker
Car heater
Ground heater.

What am I?

Brandon Beat (7)
Beaconhill Community First School, Cramlington

Kennings Poem

Snow flaker
Snowball maker
Rain freezer
Feet chiller
Ground coverer
Weather cooler
Slipper wetter
Sock wetter
Hand cooler
Heat freezer
Frost wetter
Clothes wetter
Face cooler
Dog cooler
Cat wetter
Rabbit wetter
Dog scarer.

What am I?

Aimee Nelson (7)
Beaconhill Community First School, Cramlington

Untitled

Sunshine
It is so great
So big with its bright light
I like its yellow, great bright light.

Lightning
Shoots down so fast
Sometimes makes a big fire
Makes the sky a bright light
Nice sight.

Lewis Younger (8)
Beaconhill Community First School, Cramlington

Kennings

Snow flaker
Snowball maker
Rain freezer
Feet chiller
Sock wetter
Heat freezer
Nose runner
Hand cooler
Slipper wetter
Frost creator
Ground coverer
Clothes soaker
Door breaker
Window blocker
Face cooler
Dog teaser
Cat scarer
Finger nipper.

Katrina Ouzman (8)
Beaconhill Community First School, Cramlington

Frost

Window cover
Grass freezer
Leaf nipper
Rock cover
Soil freezer
Ground nipper
Glass freezer
Plant froster
Car cover
Tree nipper.

What am I?

Olivia Sarginson (7)
Beaconhill Community First School, Cramlington

Lullaby

I have brought you a cheetah
So you will be fast
I have brought you a dog
So you will be cosy
I have brought you a lion
So you will be happy.

Liam Richardson (7)
Beaconhill Community First School, Cramlington

Kennings

Heat maker
Face burner
House burner
Snow melter
Heat riser
Body sweater
Ice cream melter
Hair burner.

What am I?

Bethany Sanderson (7)
Beaconhill Community First School, Cramlington

Lullaby

I have brought you a bib
So you will not get messy
I have brought you a unicorn
So you will fly wherever you want
You will have a pram
So you can go out with your mum.

Kayleigh Jewitt (7)
Beaconhill Community First School, Cramlington

Snowstorms

Body cooler
Tree blower
Chimney blocker
Grass shaker
Glass blower
Sweet cracker
Wind breezer
Chilly riser
Slippery slider
Ground shaker
Car cover
Frost freezer
Tree cover.

Carl Parry (8)
Beaconhill Community First School, Cramlington

Kennings Poem

Ground coverer
Snow maker
Grass freezer
Home breaker
Snow flaker
Blizzard maker
Ice maker
Snow plougher
Frost maker
Heart breaker
Sock wetter.

What am I?

Ronan S Jennings (7)
Beaconhill Community First School, Cramlington

Kennings Poem

House smasher
People shaker
Hair shaker
Roof breaker
Grass shaker
Hat blower
Tree smasher
Temperature dropper
Leaf juggler
Tree rattler

What am I?

Sean Lazonby (7)
Beaconhill Community First School, Cramlington

Lullaby

I have brought you a dummy
So you will be happy.
I will buy you a bottle
So you can drink some milk.
I have brought you a rattle
So you can put it in your hand.
I will buy you a dog
So you can play with it.
I will buy you a cat
So you can see in the dark.
You will have nice hair
Like a princess.

Shannon English (8)
Beaconhill Community First School, Cramlington

Snowball - Cinquain

Snowballs
They can hurt you
You can have fights with them
They're white as a piece of paper
Snowballs.

John Wilkinson (8)
Beaconhill Community First School, Cramlington

What Am I?

Belly rumbler
Snow melter
House burner
Ash shooter
Car melter
Steam puffer
Over heater
Earthquake creator
Tree killer.

A: volcano.

Brent Richardson (8)
Beaconhill Community First School, Cramlington

Rain Kennings

Hair drencher
Clothes wetter
Shoe soaker
Umbrella shaker
Head hitter
Puddle maker.

Caitlin McMillan (7)
Beaconhill Community First School, Cramlington

Lullaby

I have brought you a lion
So you will be brave
I have brought you a woodpecker
So you can cut trees
You will have blue eyes
So that you can see in the dark.

Connor Jackson (7)
Beaconhill Community First School, Cramlington

Snow Kennings

Angel maker
Nose nipper
Finger nipper
Blanket maker
Blizzard maker
Ice maker
Snowball maker
Ice freezer
Cat scarer
Car coverer.

Ellie Millar (7)
Beaconhill Community First School, Cramlington

Lullaby

I have brought you a pony
So you will run fast
I have brought you a dog
So you will be brave
You will have strong bones
So you can lift heavy things.

Jaimie Davison-Stewart (7)
Beaconhill Community First School, Cramlington

A Family Of Cinquains

My snake
Poos everywhere
Strangles me every day
Shed his skin every time I look
Good snake.

My bro
He is funny
He annoys my good dog
He tries to kill my dog, she's good
Bad bro.

My mam
She has nice hair
She helps me every day
She's always good with me and bro
Nice mam.

My dog
Runs everywhere
She likes me and my bro
Jumps up when I'm lying in bed
Good dog.

Me, Josh
Good for my mam
Annoy bro every day
Annoying my bro all the time
Good Josh.

Josh White (8)
Beaconhill Community First School, Cramlington

Lullaby

I have brought you a fast leopard
So you will run quickly
You have a good brain
So you will never forget
You will have a cottage to live in.

Dylan Darbyshire
Beaconhill Community First School, Cramlington

Lullaby

I have brought you a dummy
So you will never cry.
I have brought you a cat
So you can run fast.
I have brought you a dog
So you can jump.
You will have blue eyes
So you can have night vision.

Mathew Davidson (7)
Beaconhill Community First School, Cramlington

Lullaby

I have brought you a cot
So you will have somewhere to sleep.
I have brought you a cat
So you will be good at jumping.
I have brought you a playmate
So you will have fun.
You will have a good mind
So that you will never forget.

Ki Green (7)
Beaconhill Community First School, Cramlington

Lullaby

I have brought you a dummy
So you will be quiet
I have brought you a cat
So it will keep you happy
You will have beautiful hands
So that you can write.

Courtney Thompson (7)
Beaconhill Community First School, Cramlington

Lullaby

I have brought you a horse
So you will be fast
I have brought you a teddy
So you will be happy
You will have blond hair
So you will look beautiful.

John Abbott (7)
Beaconhill Community First School, Cramlington

Lullaby

I have brought you a cot
So you will be able to sleep.
I have brought you a bottle
So you will not get thirsty.
I have brought you a cute dress
For when you get christened.
You will have blonde hair
So you will look lovely.

Nikita Stephenson (7)
Beaconhill Community First School, Cramlington

Lullaby

I have brought you a dog
So you will run fast
I have brought you a nappy
So you will be dry
You will have beautiful ears
So that you can listen well.

Jack Hindle (8)
Beaconhill Community First School, Cramlington

A Family Of Cinquains

Darcy
He's chocolate
He is very bouncy
He chases the cat for fun fights
Nitwit

Aimèe
She is dead now
I loved my big sister
My sister was very lovely
Miss her

Eryne
She's beautiful
I am her godfather
I was chosen by my aunty
Lovely

Kieren
He is naughty
He is very skinny
He is so naughty at Beavers
Big bum

Mummy
I love her lots
She is so pretty and
She is a shop freak at shops, that's
Mummy

Daddy
Is a trainer
Not the one on our feet
The one that trains a dog, my dog
Darcy.

Joseph Luke (8)
Beaconhill Community First School, Cramlington

A Family Of Cinquains

Lucy
My big sister
Sometimes nasty to me
Won't go to bed at the same time
Not nice.

Joanne
Little sister
Is nearly four months old
Tubes up her nose in hospital
Fine now.

Ryan
Little brother
He is cute when he cries
He turns over in the bath now
Tinker.

My mam
She cooks my food
Her cooking is super
Finds my Tamagotchi for me
Lovely.

Bonnie
She is bonnie
She sleeps under the cot
Her birthday is after mine, cool
Spooky.

Cassie
She is my dog
Loves outside, the fresh air
Chases the torchlight round and round
Funny.

Charlotte Perry (8)
Beaconhill Community First School, Cramlington

My Family Of Cinquains

Megan
My little sis
Never stops butting in
Small but she is a 'whinge-a-lot'
Sister.

My bro
Screams every day
He is the best brother
Makes a lot of noise at bedtime
My bro.

My mam
Makes my packed lunch
Gives me water for school
Lets me play over at Ashleigh's
My mum.

My dad
Makes pipes at work
Works in a factory
He likes to watch the band practice
My dad.

Rabbit
Fast at running
Likes to scratch me a lot
Her name is Rose, she likes to run
Rabbit.

Flownder
Swims in his tank
Flownder likes his fish food
He is now my favourite fish
Swimming.

Laurie Bramwell (8)
Beaconhill Community First School, Cramlington

My Family Of Cinquains

My bro
He is Aidan
He likes to pick his nose
His bedroom is always a tip
Bad boy!

My mam
Likes her hot tea
Always in the garden
She hates to pick the dog's poo up!
Smelly!

Grandma
She hates the dog
Has a humongous bed
She has a telly in her room!
Loves it!

My dad
Lives in Cyprus
He always snorts in bed
He loves to go and shop for beer
Boozy!

Kelly
She's got a dog
She likes to play with hair
My aunt she is a total nut
Crazy!

My pet
He is the best
Has two walks every day
He is a very mucky pup
Is lush!

Courtney Egerton (8)
Beaconhill Community First School, Cramlington

A Family Of Cinquains

Sister!
She hates all sprouts
She likes to pick her nose
My sister is nasty and sly.
Chicken!

My mum
Good at cooking
Very cool at looking
My mum is lazy and funny.
Wicked!

Grandma
Always lovely
She used to have two dogs
She has a very big house cool.
Awesome!

Cousin
She is bossy
Sometimes is in my way
Like to fight with nasty cousin.
Meany!

Doggy
Big and fluffy
He likes to bark a lot
He loves to have dog chews a lot
That's him!

Aaron
He cries a lot
He has big poos and pumps
And has loads of toys to play with.
Aaron!

Callum Nelson (8)
Beaconhill Community First School, Cramlington

A Family Of Cinquains

Holly
She is gentle
She goes behind the shed
She likes to lick people's faces
Silly.

Matthew
Loves to kiss Sam
Matthew really loves me
He is so rough, he's left scratches.
Solid.

Daniel
So annoying
He always plays with me
He helps me put the rabbits in.
Crazy.

My mam
She loves Chinese
Her favourite is curry
She likes spaghetti bolognese
Greedy!

Ripple
Naughty rabbit
She was born at Easter
She is a psychotic rabbit
Silly.

My dad
He is silly
He really does love me
He leaves the door open at night.
Fatty!

Abbie Paxton (7)
Beaconhill Community First School, Cramlington

A Family - Cinquains

Buster
Slavery dog
Big, white and furry thing
Can kill you if he wanted to
Bad dog!

Sasha
Lovely Staffy
Loves to chew on thick wood
Beautiful little dog, cute girl
Good dog!

Smoky
Big fat hairball
Always licking her fur
Does her business in my bedroom
That's her!

Babies
His name is Shaun
He always cries for me
Now he is crawling all the time
Save me!

Sister
My Niomme
She makes me so tired
She loves curry so very much
Sisters.

Shannon Fantozzi (8)
Beaconhill Community First School, Cramlington

My Family Of Cinquains

Sister
So annoying
She always fights with me
Hates casserole and vegetables
Silly.

My mum
Really fussy
Really loves animals
Used to have five cats and two rats
Lovely.

My pet
Really greedy
That's why he is so fat
Fights with my other guinea pig
Called Crush.

Chloe
My sweet cousin
Sometimes really bossy
But really nice and cares for us
So sweet.

Jordan
Really noisy
He is in a wheelchair
He is a brilliant driver
Poor boy.

Nanna
So kind to us
She cares for us a lot
We do lots of kind stuff for her
Lovely.

Courtney Lamb (8)
Beaconhill Community First School, Cramlington

A Family Of Cinquains

Budgie
He always poops
He really hates balloons
He is always singing my name
Old bird.

My mam
See her at school
She watches EastEnders
She never stops going shopping.
Boring.

My sis
Never shuts up
She's very annoying
She's the size of a four-year-old
Weird.

My dad
He's brilliant
Once went to Singapore
He was a model car racer
Strange man.

Cassie
My cousin's dog
She goes camping with us
She always does as she is told
Good girl.

Gannie
She's ninety now
She lived during the war
Her husband was in World War II.
She's great.

Thomas Jewitt (8)
Beaconhill Community First School, Cramlington

A Family Of Cinquains

Sister!
Is annoying
Fights with me all the time.
She tried to take my ted's ear off.
Hate her.

Poppy!
Is really cute
She dug down to a pipe.
She was named after a flower.
So cute.

Daddy!
Is so lovely
Works at GNER
He does not support Newcastle.
Lovely.

Lewis!
Goes to Brockwell
Plays mini golf with me
He is so so so kind to me
Nice boy.

Mammy!
She cooks nice food
She does like the football
She cleans up the dog's sick and poo.
Good Mam.

Michael!
Is annoying
Pulled my teddy's head off
He works at a garden centre.
Nasty.

George Tweddell Brown (8)
Beaconhill Community First School, Cramlington

A Family Of Cinquains!

My mam!
She's the greatest
She never stops shopping
She watches 'Coronation Street'.
Lovely.

Uncle!
His name is Chris.
Always goes to the pub
He is trying to stop smoking.
Cool guy.

My dad!
He's very fat
He is a bit crazy.
I think he's the best dad ever.
Silly.

My dog!
What a monkey
He loves greasy fat bones
He licks Treasure's bowl when she's out.
Crazy.

Katie!
She's my sister
She is really ugly
She always shouts at me all day.
The brat.

My gran!
She loves to sew
Makes nice things for my tea
She looks after me and my sis.
Best gran.

Cameron Scott (7)
Beaconhill Community First School, Cramlington

A Family Of Cinquains

My cat
She is mental
She always annoys me
She always whinges for her food
Greedy!

My dad
He is hyper
He watches 'Most Haunted'
He eats too much food at bedtime
Silly!

My mum
She is naughty
She has a smelly bed
She likes to shop for boots and bags
Sweetie.

Sister
She is stupid
She is always hungry
She doesn't like going to bed
Hungry.

My bro
Screams all the time
Gives me a bad headache
He is hungry like my sister
Cool dude.

Grandma
She is so kind
She likes wine and brandy
She is a fashion designer
Lovely.

Siobhan Wilkinson (9)
Beaconhill Community First School, Cramlington

A Family Of Cinquains

Brandon!
Always fighting
Always playing football
Brandon is a pain in the butt
That's him!

My mam!
She is so kind
Helps me with my homework
My mam makes good Sunday dinners
She's mad!

My dad!
He is crazy
He goes to Spain and France
He makes me happy when I'm sad
Nice dad!

My sis!
She is so mad
She is a mad sister
My sister hates spicy curry.
Crazy.

My cat!
He's called Libra
He scratches me a lot
He loves me because I feed him
My cat!

My Karl!
He loves TV
Always out in the town
He also loves his computer
Bad boy!

Ashleigh Beat (8)
Beaconhill Community First School, Cramlington

Acrostic Poem

S un is very bright
U nless the clouds come out and it starts to rain
N early every sunny day we can play
N obody wants to play when it rains
Y es, you can go to the beach every sunny

D ay, but rainy days the sand gets wet
A nd so does the rocks and you can hear the birds
Y eilling and
S inging.

Demi-Lee Marshall (7)
Beaconhill Community First School, Cramlington

Acrostic Poem

S un in the sky falls down on the ground
U nlike the wind in the sky
N ear the morning the sun rises
N ear the night the sun sets
Y ear after year summer is bright.

D ay after day is very light
A nd the sun in summer makes people get swimming
Y ears are cool with summer
S eason after season brings a new spring.

Sarah-Louise Young (7)
Beaconhill Community First School, Cramlington

I Was Late Because . . .

I was late because my mum's car broke down
I was late because I walked to town
I was late because I got lost
I was late because I got stuck in a heap of compost
I was late because I broke my leg
I was late because I got hung up by a peg
I was late because I fell in a lake
I was late because I went home and baked a cake
I was late because my watch was broken
I was late because I saw a token
I was late because I wandered into the sea
I was late because I got chased by a chimpanzee.

Katie Webb (7)
Bromham CE Lower School, Bromham

Fireworks

It is sparkly
It is magic
It has different colours
And it has lovely colours
It is pretty
It makes me happy
It is burning hot
It is lovely
It is very noisy
It makes you say *wow!*

Jordan Warwick (7)
Bromham CE Lower School, Bromham

I Was Late Because . . .

I was late because
I got lost.
I was late because
I froze from frost.
I was late because
I fell into a lake.
I was late because
I got my foot stuck in a rake.
I was late because
I wandered into the sea.
I was late because
A bee stung me.
I was late because
Three lions came out of nowhere.
I was late because
They were just over there.
I was late because
I stopped and picked my nose.
I was late because
I took a very long doze.

Chloe Preston (8)
Bromham CE Lower School, Bromham

Yesterday I . . .

Yesterday I went to the park
Yesterday I saw a shark
Yesterday I went to the North Pole
Yesterday I fell down a hole
Yesterday I went to bed
Yesterday I bumped my head
Yesterday I went to the moon
Yesterday I found a spoon
Yesterday I saw a frog
Yesterday I saw a dog.

Marley Newland (7)
Bromham CE Lower School, Bromham

I Didn't Go To Sleep Because . . .

I did not go to sleep because
I heard funny noises.
I did not go to sleep because
I heard whishing wind.
I did not go to sleep because
I heard someone coming.
I did not go to sleep because
I heard my mum flush the toilet.
I did not go to sleep because
I heard the doorbell ring.
I did not go to sleep because
I heard a burglar coming in.
I did not go to sleep because
I heard a ghost at the window.

Emma Patrickson (8)
Bromham CE Lower School, Bromham

I Didn't Go To Sleep Because . . .

I didn't go to sleep because I thought I heard funny noises
I didn't go to sleep because I heard the owl singing
I didn't go to sleep because I heard the rhinoceros humming
I didn't go to sleep because I heard the rain raining
I didn't go to sleep because I heard the toilet flushing
I didn't go to sleep because I heard the trees fighting
I didn't go to sleep because I heard my dad snoring
I didn't go to sleep because I heard something in my wardrobe
I didn't go to sleep because I heard the teacher hooting
I didn't go to sleep because I heard someone coming
I didn't go to sleep because I felt something pushing my bed
I didn't go to sleep because I heard the blackboard swaying
I didn't go to sleep because I heard my bed talking.

Megan Wallace (7)
Bromham CE Lower School, Bromham

I Stayed In My Bedroom Because . . .

I stayed in my bedroom because
My cat was sitting on my feet.
I stayed in my bedroom because
I fell out of bed.
I stayed in my bedroom because
There was a gigantic spider in the hall.
I stayed in my bedroom because
I wanted to break the bed.
I stayed in my bedroom because
A monster was in the hall.
I stayed in my bedroom because
There was a bomb outside my bedroom.
I stayed in my bedroom because
A traffic jam was in the hall.
I stayed in my bedroom because
Outside was a fireball!

James Gillum (8)
Bromham CE Lower School, Bromham

Yesterday I . . .

Yesterday I was in the dark
Yesterday I was eaten by a shark
Yesterday I went to the moon
Yesterday I was eating with a spoon
Yesterday I went in a rocket
Yesterday I put my hand in my pocket
Yesterday I bought a cat
Yesterday I chased a bat
Yesterday I was bashing my head
Yesterday I was eating instead.

James Thomson (7)
Bromham CE Lower School, Bromham

There's A Hole In My Bag Because . . .

There's a hole in my bag because
The dog chewed it up.
There's a hole in my bag because
I left it with his pup.
There's a hole in my bag because
I left a knife in it.
There's a hole in my bag because
I dropped it in a quarry pit.
There's a hole in my bag because
I picked a loose thread.
There's a hole in my bag because
I trusted my friend, Ned.
There's a hole in my bag because
It got trapped in the door.
There's a hole in my bag because
I dropped it on a spiky floor.
There's a hole in my bag because
I included it in shaving my hair.
There's a hole in my bag because
The razor gave me quite a scare!

Joe Tebbett (8)
Bromham CE Lower School, Bromham

Tigers

A tiger is orange as a carrot.
A tiger jumps as high as a kangaroo.
Tigers pounce and growl.
Fire eyes sparkle at night.
Tigers are prowling in the night.
Tigers' teeth are sharp as razors.

Ben Hammond (7)
Bromham CE Lower School, Bromham

A Rocket

White paint
Extreme power
Fuel as hot as a fireball
Very fast
Long countdown
Three or six fuel blasters
Fuel tanks cold as snow.

Nathan Weightman (7)
Bromham CE Lower School, Bromham

Fire

Crackling, burning
As hot as a fireplace,
A dazzling red,
Golden spreading,
Bright light fire.

James Harding (8)
Bromham CE Lower School, Bromham

I Was Late Because . . .

I was late because my sister is slow
I was late because my sister says no
I was late because I spend ages in bed
I was late because I met Fred
I was late because I had a shower
I was late because I met a flower
I was late because I made a cake
I was late because I cooked and baked.

Thomas O'Neill (7)
Bromham CE Lower School, Bromham

What School Means To Me

School begins at quarter to nine,
I hope I get there in time.
When I go through the gates,
There I meet all my mates.
We go inside, take off our coats
Get our books and compare our notes.
English, maths, RE too
These are the lessons we have to do.
Writing, drawing all day long
Then it is time to sing a song.
At 3 o'clock the lessons end
That's when I walk home with my friend.

Thomas Whitby (9)
Carmountside Primary School, Stoke-on-Trent

What School Means To Me

School means fun forever
School is now so clever
School is activities for fun
School is for things to get done
School dinners are so yummy
School is even nice for my tummy
School makes me feel happy when I step through the gate
School is not good when I'm late
School is like it never ends
School is fun now to spend
School is so crisp and cool
School is stopping me from being a fool.

Jake Britchfield (9)
Carmountside Primary School, Stoke-on-Trent

What School Means To Me

School starts at quarter to nine
School I hope will start on time.
School is running in a race
I hope I don't trip over my lace.
In my school you have to have a good thought
In my school there is a lot of sport.
I don't usually get a bad report
So I think I have been taught.
School is cool, I get to play with my mate
The bell rings, I run, I'm never late.

Bradley Hancock (8)
Carmountside Primary School, Stoke-on-Trent

What School Means To Me

School means playing with friends
School is friendship that never ends
School is cool, we don't be a fool
School is a big, gigantic pool
School is for prizes which come in shapes and sizes
School is for speaking privately, not shouting out
School is for learning forever, not wriggling about
School is for never fighting
School is usually just for writing
School is not acting like a fool
School is a place where we need tools
School is great, I'm never late
School is my best mate!

James Wright (8)
Carmountside Primary School, Stoke-on-Trent

Untitled

School makes me run if I am late
When I am there I meet my mate.
School starts at quarter to nine
I hope I get there on time.
School makes me happy, so fine
I wish I could stay there all the time.
School makes me happy if I swim my best
We always have a Friday test.
School means you make more friends
I wish my friendship never ends.

Samuel Thurston (8)
Carmountside Primary School, Stoke-on-Trent

What School Means To Me

School is playing with my mate
School is walking through the gate.
School is running in a big sport
School is having a good report.
School is watching the sky turning bright
School is switching on the light.
School is playtime being earned
School is writing and knowing you've learned.
School dinners are so nice
Especially the curry sauce with rice.

Julia Unwin (9)
Carmountside Primary School, Stoke-on-Trent

What School Means To Me

School is cool
Don't play the fool
School is funny
School is sweet like honey
The teachers are nice
The kids are twice
The school poems rhyme
So we have good times
The nursery children are all new
The Y6 are the oldest, quite a few.

Kieron Thompson (8)
Carmountside Primary School, Stoke-on-Trent

What School Means To Me

School dinners make me full,
School will never be dull.
Teachers are all different shapes and sizes,
Teachers are for helping and giving prizes.
School means playing with my friend,
School means my friendship will never end.
School teaches me sport
And I never get a bad report.
School has a good rule,
School stops me playing the fool.
School will be there each day,
School will never go away.

Bradley Stevenson (9)
Carmountside Primary School, Stoke-on-Trent

Moving People

Everybody eats
And people meet,
Babies cry,
People die,
You look
At a book,
I walk,
We all talk,
We get dressed
And put on a vest,
Some are good
And some aren't understood.

Tonicha Brett (9)
Carmountside Primary School, Stoke-on-Trent

What School Means To Me

School is not for being late,
School is for coming with my mate.
School rules are so great,
School makes me never late.
School is fun forever,
School is now making me clever.
School is activities for learning fun,
School is for things to get done.
School is so, so, so, so cool,
School stops me from becoming a fool.

Hollie Munday (8)
Carmountside Primary School, Stoke-on-Trent

What School Means To Me

School is good education
School has a good location
School is earning prizes
School prizes are all shapes and sizes
School teachers are lots of fun
School teachers nag at you to get your work done
School is all about friends
School friendship never ends
But school rules
And it's cool!
So don't forget
And don't play the fool!

Rebecca Matthews (8)
Carmountside Primary School, Stoke-on-Trent

What School Means To Me

School means playing with mates
School means I never arrive late
School time is fun, ever so short
School is not for a bad report
School is never letting yourself down
School means working, not being a clown
School is now so clever
School has activities forever
School is for getting things done
School is now for work and fun
School is there for everyone
Home time comes and I am gone!

Reegan Harvey (8)
Carmountside Primary School, Stoke-on-Trent

What School Means To Me

School starts at quarter to nine
I hope I get there on time.
When I get through the gates
I meet all my mates.
School pudding is so nice
But I especially like the rice.
We go inside, take off our coats
Get our books and compare our notes.
These are the lessons we have to do
English, maths, RE too.
Writing, drawing all day long
Then it is time to sing a song.
At 3 o'clock the lessons end
That's when I walk home with a friend.

Molly Newton (8)
Carmountside Primary School, Stoke-on-Trent

What School Means To Me

School rules
I enjoy the day
When I pay my dinner money
I always want to stay
School teachers are nice
Kids are twice as nice!
When I go home at night
I am always out of sight
But when I am at school
I am never a fool.

Christian Longshaw (8)
Carmountside Primary School, Stoke-on-Trent

What School Means To Me

School means to help each other,
School means do not bully one another.
School is for having fun,
School is for playing in the sun.
School dinners are so tasty,
The apple pie is made from pastry.
School is for not being late,
School is for helping my best mate.
School is for eating healthy food,
School is not for getting in a mood.
School means to learn and play,
School means to have a nice day!

Sharna Baskerville (8)
Carmountside Primary School, Stoke-on-Trent

Volcano

A volcano is . . .

    Red, pure blood
        Black death
            A steamy kettle
                Hot air
                    A loud crash
                        A topless mountain

    A bottomless hole
        A dead place
            A sad place
                A night place
                    A destroyer of cities
                    A killer of man
                      A cruel place
                        The darkest dark

No-man's land
    Evil.

Scott Shaw (11)
Cumbernauld Primary School, Cumbernauld

A Diamond Is . . .

A cluster of moonbeams
A star in disguise
A mosaic of mirrors
A sparkle in a blind man's eye
A shimmering bubble
A palm in an evergreen forest
Desire
Destiny
Peace.

Fiona Dalling (10)
Cumbernauld Primary School, Cumbernauld

Winter

The snow is a big bowl of vanilla ice cream,
The snowmen are big snow people in the snow,
Hot chocolate is a cup of brown, thick snow,
The frozen water is diamonds in a mine,
Snowballs are big Maltesers falling from the sky.

Kara Graham (10)
Cumbernauld Primary School, Cumbernauld

The Perfect Gift

If I could, I would give you . . .
A gazillion pounds
A house made of chocolate
Hair made from candyfloss
A flying Ferrari
An everlasting hug
A yacht that floats in space
A monkey
A life of luxury
A day of eating cheese with Wallace and Grommit
A never-breaking heart.

Fraser Doyle (10)
Cumbernauld Primary School, Cumbernauld

The Perfect Gift

If I could I would give you . . .
A private yacht so you can come visit
A money tree to grow in your back garden
A shiny star to keep in your pocket
A trip around the world and back
A solid gold mansion
And eternal friendship.

Olivia Roxburgh-Begg (10)
Cumbernauld Primary School, Cumbernauld

The Perfect Gift

A child with a heart of gold to hold and love forever
        Hope
Contagious smiles
A room made of rubies and flashing diamonds
A birthday every day
        Love
A world made of teddy bears
Fresh water and
        Peace.

Laura Campbell (10)
Cumbernauld Primary School, Cumbernauld

The Jungle Is . . .

A monkey's playground
A lion's castle
A snake's home
A tree's paradise
A bird's haven
A cheetah's racetrack.

Andrew Norman (10)
Cumbernauld Primary School, Cumbernauld

The Perfect Gift

If I could I would give you . . .
All the money in the world
A bed the size of China
A Ferrari gleaming in the sun
A jumbo jet of gold
The power to feed the world
Scotland to win the World Cup
A bronze speedboat
A cure for cancer
A silver limo as shiny as the sun
All the friends you want
A sunny day in Scotland
Eternal life.

Jordan Maclean (10)
Cumbernauld Primary School, Cumbernauld

The Perfect Gift

If I could I would give you . . .
A cruise around the world
A friendly baby snake
A house made of sweets
Hair made of chocolate
An everlasting life
A seat on top of the world
A trip to Spain
A bed the size of the world
A body made of sweets
An everlasting hug
An 11 million miles per hour Subaru
A never-breaking heart.

Rebecca Blair (10)
Cumbernauld Primary School, Cumbernauld

The Perfect Gift

If I could, I would give you . . .

World peace,
A jumbo jet to travel into space,
A family to grow happy and active,
A winning lottery ticket,
Ricky Gervais as a best friend,
A private box at Ibrox,
Everlasting crisps,
The power to make poverty history,
Free sports channels,
The ability to play football without breaking your arm,
Long life for children,
A nice, helpful, not bossy boss,
Everlasting friendship.

Paige Mitchelson (10)
Cumbernauld Primary School, Cumbernauld

The Perfect Gift

If I could, I would give you . . .
The peace of the world
The glistening stars of the sky
Eternal life
A family so grand
Bombs to disappear
A trip to the sun
The moon in your hands
End of world poverty
The hippy era to come back
The beauty of Kirsty Hume
Africa without poverty
An everlasting smile.

Samantha Davidson (10)
Cumbernauld Primary School, Cumbernauld

A Smile

A smile is delightful,
A smile is fun,
A smile is a big, big hug
From your mum.

A smile is cheesy,
A smile's a grin,
You could not dare to
Throw that smile in the bin.

A smile's life,
A smile's love,
A smile's like
Clouds and Heaven above.

Hannah Johnstone (10)
Cumbernauld Primary School, Cumbernauld

The Perfect Gift

If I could I would give you . . .
A pink, metallic Porsche with a Jacuzzi in the back
A fountain of chocolate
A self-cleaning bedroom
The biggest bed in the world
A CD with the best rave music
A cupboard full of sweets
A solid gold TV
Fun in every corner
Eternal friendship.

Cara Dalziel (10)
Cumbernauld Primary School, Cumbernauld

Christmas

C hildren filled with Christmas joy
H olly brightly sitting on a bush
R iver hardened into a pool of diamonds
I cicles sparkling like glass
S tars hanging in the sky like decorations on the tree
T rees glittered with sparkling snow
M oonlight spreading across the houses
A quilt of snow lying on the frozen grass
S weetly coloured presents waiting under the tree.

Olivia Bryant (10)
Cumbernauld Primary School, Cumbernauld

A Volcano Is . . .

A magma machine gun on a rampage
A runny fire chamber
A hot hole
Attracting heat magnet
Two boys in a fight
Fire bomb dropping from the sky
A volcano is a gold liquid.

Ryan Dukes (10)
Cumbernauld Primary School, Cumbernauld

The Perfect Gift

If I could, I would give you . . .
The power to win The Open at St Andrews,
An everlasting life,
World peace,
The chance to see your grandchildren,
£10,000,
The moon and stars,
An end to poverty,
The world.

Sophie Thomson (10)
Cumbernauld Primary School, Cumbernauld

A Perfect Gift

(To Mum from Amy)

If I could, I would give you . . .
Sunshine every day,
A beach for a back garden,
A waterfall of happiness,
The power to hypnotise your children to make them tidy their rooms,
A load of fun for everyone,
A fluffy cloud to relax on,
A child to hug,
An everlasting pack of digestive biscuits to dip in your tea,
A lady who pampers you every day,
To stop world hunger,
Everything there is to give.

Amy Sutherland (10)
Cumbernauld Primary School, Cumbernauld

Christmas

C hristmas fire blazing in the silent night
H eavy snow covering the ground like a soft baby's blanket
R inging bells echoing in the distance like the thunder's roar
 I cy lights gleaming like multicoloured stars
S tockings hanging, waiting to be filled, like a bird waiting for food
T rees standing and showing off like a model on a catwalk
M ulticoloured presents crinkling when you touch them
A nnoying children grabbing at the candy canes like they've never
been fed
S nowmen gazing at the bright pink sky gleaming in front of them.

Kayleigh Standish (10)
Cumbernauld Primary School, Cumbernauld

The Perfect Gift

If I could, I would give you . . .

A bowl of cereal the size of a house,
Everlasting hair gel,
Golden football boots with the skills of the world's best football player
And the speed of a Ferrari,
A book of knowledge,
The biggest bed in the world,
One million pounds to spend on whatever you want,
A private jet to take you wherever your heart desires,
The world's biggest football pitch in your back garden,
A leprechaun to give you hopes and dreams,
Sweets that are healthy,
A spot-free face,
A huge, cuddly teddy bear to hug when you're lonely.

Claudia Smith (10)
Cumbernauld Primary School, Cumbernauld

The Jungle Is . . .

A shark-free land
A tiger's buffet
An elephant's bath
A monkey's heaven
A rhino's rampage ground
Tarzan's home
A green blanket
A lion's battlefield.

Ben Chok (9)
Cumbernauld Primary School, Cumbernauld

A Perfect Gift

If I could, I would give you . . .

A garden of colour
A body that heals
A house of love
A mum to cuddle
A breath of fresh air
A royal walk on top of the world
A husband to care for you
God's kiss goodnight

A peaceful life.

Kerrie Campbell (10)
Cumbernauld Primary School, Cumbernauld

Sky

The sky is . . .
God's home
The stars' city
A sheet of blue
Home to the sun and moon
A cloud-covered surface of candyfloss
A plane's road
The barrier between Earth and space
Our view when we look up
An artist's dream
A place we cannot enter.

Nadia Wilson (10)
Cumbernauld Primary School, Cumbernauld

The Perfect Gift

If I could, I would give you . . .

Sunshine in Scotland,
A ring with a diamond the size of a candle,
A heart of gold,
A white, stretch limo with a hot tub and a mini bar,
A diamond wedding,
Fame, glamour and money,
A huge house in Spain,
All the money in the world,
A trip to *Heaven!*

Amanda Valentine (10)
Cumbernauld Primary School, Cumbernauld

A Perfect Gift

If I could, I would give you . . .

A chance to live on top of the world,
A pot full of gold,
A trip around the world,
A child of your own,
An everlasting box of chocolates,
A nice, healthy family,
An angel of love.

Stephanie Minnes (9)
Cumbernauld Primary School, Cumbernauld

War Is . . .

War is full of howling bombs
War is soldiers scurrying like ants
War is bloody rivers in the trenches

War is trenches full of blood
War is howling planes
War is full of drizzling bombs

War is full of bombs twirling around
War is full of bombs screaming
War is full of people shooting the sky

War is harsh rationing books
War is a lonely suitcase
War is full of muddy blood.

Matthew Frost (9)
Elworth Hall Primary School, Sandbach

War Is . . .

War is a lonely suitcase
War is anxious teddies
War is rivers of blood
War is men falling down a hill like rabbits
War is a screaming train
War is an air raid siren howling like a dog
War is bombs dropping like a man hammering a nail
War is scared planes
War is worried bombs
War is sad trenches
War is crying tanks
War is soldiers like bulldogs.

Thomas Wilson (10)
Elworth Hall Primary School, Sandbach

War Is . . .

War is crying evacuees
War is lonely teddies
War is anxious suitcases

War is crying evacuees
War is upset evacuees
War is worried evacuees

War is crying evacuees
War is letters sad and shy
War is frightened apple pie

War is crying evacuees
War is tired clothes
War is courageous photos

War is crying evacuees
War is ID cards checking in
War is unhappy gas masks

War is crying evacuees.

Sarah Evans (9)
Elworth Hall Primary School, Sandbach

War Is . . .

War is lonely suitcases
War is anxious teddies
War is rivers of blood
War is men falling, falling down like rabbits in a field
War is a screaming train with evacuees on it
War is scared planes
War is worried bombs
War is trenches of unhappiness
War is crying tanks
War is soldiers like bulldogs.

Daniel Powell (9)
Elworth Hall Primary School, Sandbach

War Is . . .

War is crying evacuees,
War is lonely suitcases,
War is anxious teddies,
War is shy evacuees,
War is worried mums,
War is a sad suitcase,
War is afraid children,
War is tatty children's clothes,
War is air raid sirens,
War is curious dads,
War is tanks running like lions,
War is evil approaching,
War is bombs dropped near the gate,
War is planes screaming through the air,
War is tanks flying through the air,
War is a billeting officer.

Rachel Shufflebotham (9)
Elworth Hall Primary School, Sandbach

War Is . . .

War is bloody rivers in the trenches
War is full of howling bombs
War is soldiers scurrying like ants
War is evil approaching
War is planes screaming through the air
War is full of muddy blood
War is full of unhappy soldiers
War is full of drizzling bombs
War is full of lonely suitcases
War is full of bombs in the distance
War is pleased chocolate.

Frankie Potter (9)
Elworth Hall Primary School, Sandbach

War Is . . .

War is lonely suitcases
War is anxious teddies
War is trenches full of men facing deadly guns
War is trenches full of bloody streams
War is bombs howling through the air
War is evil approaching
War is bombs dropped near the gate
War is planes screaming through the air
War is tanks flying through the battlefields
War is evacuees whizzing through their letters
War is afraid children
War is crying, scared evacuees
War is mouldy ration food.

Chris Stroud (10)
Elworth Hall Primary School, Sandbach

War Is . . .

War is lonely suitcases
War is anxious trains
War is crying teddies
War is empty children
War is curious teddies
War is dying fathers
War is terrified ID cards
War is trains scurrying like ants
War is mean adults like tigers prowling
War is scared apple pies
War is anxious evacuees
War is howling bombs
War is evil approaching.

Oliver Thompson (9)
Elworth Hall Primary School, Sandbach

Christmas

Christmas is blue, grey and snowy white.
It tastes like red wine and Christmas pud.
I can see snowflakes falling from the bright blue sky.
It smells like roast dinners and turkey
I can feel the cold ice on the cars
And the snow on the grass that makes a *crunch, crunch, crunch.*
I feel cold, ecstatic and excited for Christmas.

Jasmine Harland (9)
Garswood Primary School, Garswood

Untitled

Santa's cat
is as brown as a bat
his sleigh is
red just like his bed
his reindeer's
nose is as long as a hose
his beard is
as white as a candle's light.

Chloe Ratcliffe-Cross (9)
Garswood Primary School, Garswood

Friends

F riends are respectful and caring
R espect your friends
I have lots of friends
E verybody is happy
N ever hurt them
D oing things with them
S uper friends are very kind.

Francesca Miller (9)
Garswood Primary School, Garswood

The Haunted House

When I went up to this house one day
I walked up to the door and knocked
There was no answer and I wasn't surprised
Because the door to the house was blocked.
When I finally got inside
I saw to my dismay
A vampire bat with fangs
And a wonderful bird of prey.

Then came an eerie noise
From the attic up above my head
It sounded like a person
But I knew right away he was dead.
From his fingers to his toes
He was as ugly as can be
He jumped towards me laughing
'What a lovely meal for me.'

I wasn't going to be dinner
Tonight or any other
I quickly ran and ran
Back home to see my mother.

Amy Baker (9)
Garswood Primary School, Garswood

Christmas

C hristmas is when all the snow starts to fall
H eaps of snow is falling onto the walls
R udolph's nose is shining so bright
 I n the calm, starry night
S nowflakes falling from the clear sky
T here's lots of mince pies. My bedtime comes and I'm wide awake
M um's making pudding
A roma, it smells nice
S ay goodbye to autumn, hello to Christmas.

Heather Chadwick (8)
Garswood Primary School, Garswood

At The Beach

It's nice, yellow and brown,
It tastes like water and ice cream,
It sounds like the sea swishing,
It looks calming,
It smells like sausages and bacon,
It makes me feel excited.

Matthew Nolan (9)
Garswood Primary School, Garswood

Christmas

C hristmas is a time for everyone to be cheerful
H ere is Christmas, it is time to snow
R eindeers ride upon Santa's sleigh
I f you like your presents, you will play with them
S nowflakes are falling on the ground
T ime to have a little bit of fun
M ums make lovely mince pies for Christmas
A nd you get to give all your relations Christmas cards
S nowy Christmas is really here!

Sophie Spanner (8)
Garswood Primary School, Garswood

Friends

F riends are for caring and sharing things too
R acing you and having fun
I enjoy playing football with them
E veryone playing together
N ever unkind
D oing puzzles together
S o helpful!

Jake Blackburn
Garswood Primary School, Garswood

Our Horse, Maric - Cinquains

Maric,
A newborn foal,
He's a beautiful horse,
He's learning to walk steadily,
Maric.

Maric,
Racing quickly,
Speeding down the racetrack,
Galloping as fast as lightning,
Maric.

Maric,
Retired now,
He wasn't fast enough,
Now our family's special friend,
Maric.

Megan Seaman (11)
Garswood Primary School, Garswood

Spring

Spring is the time of year
I always have fun.
Running round the garden
Playing peek-a-boo.
I love to watch
The flowers grow
In the golden sun.
Night-time is quite cold
But not freezing.
I love to play in the garden
Spring is great.

Sophie Atherton (9)
Garswood Primary School, Garswood

The Moon

A big, fat football
A glowing coin in the sky
A massive wheel rim
A shiny disco ball
A big clock
A massive face
A cheese sauce ball
A big, round, whiteboard
A big, massive medal
A shining light bulb
A piece of cheese
A huge CD collection
The moon.

Joe Donovan (11)
Garswood Primary School, Garswood

The Dog

Is a . . .

    Hairy hoover
For all your leftover chips

    Muddy paws
From playing in the garden

    Floppy ears
Because that's how she is made

    Garden digger
Patrolling for a bone

    Post deliverer
She likes to give a helping paw!

Lucy Robinson (11)
Garswood Primary School, Garswood

The Cat

The cat that sits,
The cat that stares,
The cat that eats,
The cat that glares,
The cat that sleeps,
    I wonder what
        else
            he can
                do!

The cat that roars,
The cat that snores,
The cat that drinks,
The cat that winks,
The cat that licks,
The cat that loves
And the cat that cares,
    That is all
        a cat
            can
                do!

Caitlin Hewitt (11)
Garswood Primary School, Garswood

My Friends

My friends are kind
My friends are caring
My friends are funny
My friends are considerate
My friends are helpful
My friends are always smiling
My friends are respectful
My friends are sharing
My friends are not bullies
My friends are not selfish.

Amy Reeves (9)
Garswood Primary School, Garswood

Love Poem

Love, you are always here for me.
Love, I want to thank you.
Love, you gave me no fear.
Love, you will never give me a tear.
Love, you have always taken care of me.
Love, you made me so free.

Love, I want to thank you
For doing everything for me.

Laura Fletcher
Garswood Primary School, Garswood

Winter

Snowflakes falling on my face,
Outside can be such a beautiful place,
Christmas is the best time of the year,
Because of generosity, love and no fear.

Elicia-May Donlevy (9)
Garswood Primary School, Garswood

Hallowe'en

It's Hallowe'en, the night
Of the witches, children
Knocking on doors, playing
Trick or treat, it's spooky.

People lighting bonfires
Lots of cheering
Through the night
The night growing darker
Hallowe'en is *here!*

Liam Fazakerley (9)
Garswood Primary School, Garswood

Friends

My friends are kind
My friends are sweet
My friends are fast
My friends are considerate
My friends are faithful
My friends are joyful
My friends are trustworthy.

Lucy Rimmer (9)
Garswood Primary School, Garswood

Aliens!

Flying spaceships hovering in the air,
Some people are running, others stop and stare.

Yellow, red, purple and green,
Locked up in the spaceship, never to be seen!

We are lucky that we're not dead,
Snuggled up safely in our warm bed.

They stalk the night in their flying machines,
The aliens inside are never to be seen!

Jack Savage (9)
Garswood Primary School, Garswood

Winter

When it is winter
I love to play out
When it is winter
I like to mess about.

Winter is a time
When Christmas is near
Everyone has lots of Christmas cheer.

Rachael Green (9)
Garswood Primary School, Garswood

Friends

F riends are lovely
R espectful and kind
I have lots of friends like Lucy and Lindsey
E veryone is kind and
N o one is ever mean to me
D oing things with them makes me happy
S ome of them are very kind.

Rebecca Adamson
Garswood Primary School, Garswood

Colours

Red is for the red rose growing in the ground,
Yellow is for the hot sun shining in the sky,
Blue is for the bright blue sky on a summer's day,
Green is for the green grass blowing in the wind,
Pink is for the pale flowers swaying in the grass,
Brown is for the trunks of the trees standing strong and tall,
Orange is for the falling leaves in autumn all around,
Black is for empty outer space high above the Earth.

Callum Goundry (9)
Garswood Primary School, Garswood

The Tiger

The tiger rummaging in the jungle
Searching for food, *grrr!*
Suddenly, he spots something
Far away in the distance.
Can it be his prey?
The tiger creeps up silently, *chomp, chomp!*
Now he's not hungry anymore, *grrr!*

Gareth Jones (9)
Garswood Primary School, Garswood

Tiger

The tiger in the jungle, it's looking for prey,
So you'd better watch out,
Or you're the tiger's prey!

The tiger has a nap while you're reading a map,
Go the wrong way
And all that will be left
Is your cap and your map.

If you survive you will be very lucky!

Joshua Mather (9)
Garswood Primary School, Garswood

Faces

F unny faces make me laugh
A ngry faces make me mad
C ool faces make me happy
E yes on a face make me see
S miles on a face make me feel beautiful.

Megan Walsh (9)
Garswood Primary School, Garswood

What Is The Night?

The night is a black cloak
Embroidered with stars.

The night is a shadow
That covers the land.

The night is a black kitten
Dancing in the sky.

The night is a piece of paper
That's been scribbled on with a black marker.

Lauren Brown (10)
Garswood Primary School, Garswood

The Moon

The moon is a huge disco ball,
Spinning round and round.
A bright light bulb,
Shining from up above.
A giant CD collection,
Glistering in the night sky.
A piece of silver cheese,
Holey and spotty.
A shiny coin,
In my money box.

Charlotte Wiswell (11)
Garswood Primary School, Garswood

My Dad

A loving heart
A big, warm hug
A helping hand
A loving person who's always there for you
A nail that never rots
A working machine.

Jade Hough (10)
Garswood Primary School, Garswood

Kennings

A log jumper
A greedy eater
A water drinker
A great galloper
A person lover
A cuddly monster.

A horse!

Victoria Hateley (10)
Garswood Primary School, Garswood

Kennings

Shimmering light,
Spinning disk,
Shining bright,
Polished coin,
Disco ball
    The moon
    The moon

Bedtime lights
Golden pearls
Beautiful sights
Glitter scattered
Dust from Mars
    The stars
    The stars.

Collette Topping (11)
Garswood Primary School, Garswood

The Hawk

King of the sky
Like jets they fly
Soaring through the air
Searching for their prey.

Racing every bird in the world
The eagle, the owl, the falcon and winning
Swooping down to catch his prey
Then circling around his prey
Scaring off the little birds
The hawk.

Matthew Porter (10)
Garswood Primary School, Garswood

What Is A Ghost?

A ghost is a white blanket
Floating across the bedroom floor.

It is a ball of smoke
Hovering over its tombstone.

It is a ball of fog
With its head against the ceiling.

It is a white feather pillow
Waiting to smother you.

It is a sheet of white paper
Lying on the end of your bed.

But the worst thing of all is . . .
It is waiting to *scare you!*

Ashleigh Latham (10)
Garswood Primary School, Garswood

A Zombie

A zombie is:
A bog-eyed freak
An unwrapped mummy
A torn-apart doll
An uninvited guest from the graveyard
Frankenstein's cousin
Ritual beast
An alien psychopath . . .

That's a zombie!

Mark Randall (10)
Garswood Primary School, Garswood

What Is A Ghost?

A ghost is an invisible piece of paper
With no writing on it.

A ghost is a blob of mist
That floats through the graveyard.

A ghost is a misty piece of cotton wool
In a haunted castle.

A ghost is a cloud
Floating through the trees.

Jake Hamilton (10)
Garswood Primary School, Garswood

It's Christmas Time

It's Christmas time
So let's just shine
With crystal balls of snow falling from the sky
With Christmas songs here and there
It's totally Christmas everywhere.

Chelsey Thompson (10)
Garswood Primary School, Garswood

Kennings

Fun maker
A shoulder to cry on
A helping hand
A cheeky monkey
A pressie bringer
A loving teddy bear
The sun bringer.

A friend.

Lauren Austin (10)
Garswood Primary School, Garswood

What Is A Friend?

A friend is a basket full of blooming flowers,
Brightening up your day.

A friend is a mouth full of happiness,
Making you giggle.

A friend is a helping hand
For times when you're feeling down.

A friend is a light
When you're alone in the dark.

It is a shadow in the distance
As the sun rises.

A friend is a warm comfort
When you're cold.

Bethany Fairhurst (10)
Garswood Primary School, Garswood

What Is A Hedgehog?

A hedgehog is a bag of toothpicks
Sitting on the grass.

It is a spiky brush
Brushing the dirty floor.

It is a thorny bush
Rolling down the long grass.

It is a collection of sharp pencils
Waiting to be used.

It is a ball of sharp knives
Rolling off the counter.

Abbie Larkin (11)
Garswood Primary School, Garswood

What Is The Moon?

The moon is a ball of foil
Sparkling on a black piece of paper.

It is a gold coin
Dropped down a dark hole.

It is a ghostly galleon
Shining in the dark.

It is a gold thumb print
On a sheet of black paper.

It is a pot of glitter
Waiting to be used.

Ashley Smith (10)
Garswood Primary School, Garswood

What Is A Friend?

A friend is a helping hand
Always there to help you when you are stuck.

It is a string
Wrapped around you when you are upset.

A friend is forever
Following you everywhere you go.

A friend is a joker
Making you happy when you are sad.

A friend is a helper
To release you when you are stuck in a knot.

Lucy Carter (10)
Garswood Primary School, Garswood

My Dad

A beer burper,
Telly hogger,
A frustration machine,
Clever clogs,
A cuddly teddy bear,
Chelsea fanatic,
Non-stop eating machine,
Loveable monkey,
Leader of the pack,
Silly billy!

Rachel Burgess (10)
Garswood Primary School, Garswood

Monkey In The Jungle

There's a monkey in the jungle,
He's swinging from tree to tree,
He hides when someone comes
Because he doesn't want to be seen.

There's an elephant in the jungle,
He's stamping about everywhere,
He knocks down all the trees
And squirts water at me.

But there's a tiger in the jungle,
He's lurking in the long grass,
He's just jumped out at me,
So I have to run fast!

Hannah Kennedy (9)
Gorran Primary School, Coleraine

My Dog

My dog is sweet,
I love him so much,
But he loves his food more than me,
He will only play if he gets his own way,
But I love him all the same,
Because I think he is the best dog in the world!

Oliver Jamieson (10)
Gorran Primary School, Coleraine

Tractors

T ractors are fun and they do hard work
R iding in the tractor is fun
A cross the field we go with the side trailer
C ars go past the field while we are cutting the silage
T he farmer's tractors work hard
O ld tractors are smaller than new tractors
R acing tractors are fast
S o many tractors are cool!

Richard Clyde (9)
Gorran Primary School, Coleraine

Sisters

My little sister is called Rebekah,
My little sister may look cute,
But she is a real devil.
When you tell her not to come into your room, she comes in,
She jumps on you when you are trying to sleep,
If I shout at her, she goes crying to Mummy.
But when she is asleep it's Heaven!
But I have to love her.

Hannah Gault (8)
Gorran Primary School, Coleraine

My Best Teacher

My teacher is the best,
But if she is cross you're as well to stay away from her,
She knows lots of good games for PE,
She likes to drink lots of Coke, even though she knows it is bad

for you,

She has a black BMW,
I'm sure she goes very fast!
She has a black dog called Misty,
Some days she wears black clothes,
I think she must like black!
She must have lots of friends, her mobile often beeps.
If I had her number I would send her a message.
She lives at the Port and Misty enjoys the beach a lot,
I wish Misty was my dog
Because she sounds great.

Rachel Kelly (8)
Gorran Primary School, Coleraine

Upside Down World

One day I woke up and my bed was on the ceiling . . .
I fell off.
I opened my eyes to see my dog was on the roof . . .
That was just wrong.
And you know what?
He was dirty and landed on my head.
I went to the bathroom to wash up . . .
The sink was upside down
And the sewer water came out of the sink
Right on my head.
I thought it would be best to faint instead.
And when I woke up the world was back to normal!

Shane Donnelly (10)
Gorran Primary School, Coleraine

I Love Football

I love football when Liverpool are winning,
I love football when Man U are getting beat,
I love football when Rooney puts the ball high,
I love football when Rooney is sent off,
I love football because Liverpool are the best,
But most of all I love it when Cisse puts the ball
In the back of the net.

Goal!

Jamie Boreland (10)
Gorran Primary School, Coleraine

I Like Football

I like football when Man U score,
I like football when I play it with my cousins,
I like football when I play it in the rain,
I like football when I score a hat-trick,
I like football when I take penalties at my brother,
But I don't like it when my brother blocks the football on TV!

Peter Linton (9)
Gorran Primary School, Coleraine

Liverpool

L iverpool is the best team, everyone
 I n Liverpool is cool, but not as cool as Cisse
V ery cool players play for Liverpool
E veryone in the Liverpool team are cool
R eina is the best goalie for Liverpool
P eople call Steven Gerrard a brilliant player
O n Monday Liverpool won
O h! Liverpool just scored!
L uis Garcia is a right-midfielder.

Jordan Neely (9)
Gorran Primary School, Coleraine

Lion In The Jungle

There's a lion in the jungle, it's running like mad
Then I realise it's running at my dad.
There's a lion in the jungle, bad as can be
Now it's eating my friend, Lee.

There's a crocodile in the jungle
I've been running for a mile,
But when I look back again it's got a great big smile.

There's a monkey in the jungle
Swinging from tree to tree,
Oh no, that monkey's looking at me.

There's a hippo in the jungle
Bathing in the swamps,
Oh, he looks like he's down in the dumps.

There's an elephant in the jungle
And I'm not going to wait and see
What that elephant is going to do to me.

Those animals in the jungle
As far as I can see,
Seem to be waving goodbye to me.

Shanden McDowell (10)
Gorran Primary School, Coleraine

Motorbikes

M otorbikes are very good and they are cool
O n the motorbikes the men get, and go with a *zoom*
T he motorbikes rev on the track
O n they go, with their tyres spinning
R acing down the highway they go
B urn rubber on the track
I n the driver gets and the flames come out
K ick start too fast on the motorbikes
E verything about motorbikes is cool.

Timothy McNeill (9)
Gorran Primary School, Coleraine

My Family

Brothers!
Brothers are annoying,
They drive me up the wall,
They pull my hair.

Cousins!
Cousins are annoying,
They are just like brothers,
They play tricks on you.

Friends!
Friends are annoying,
They tell tales on you.

Mums!
Mums are annoying,
They make you tidy your room!

But I still love them all the same!

Nicole Boreland (8)
Gorran Primary School, Coleraine

My Cat, Fluffy

My cat Fluffy,
She's a lovely cat,
On Saturday mornings,
Dad lets her in.
She comes up to my bedroom
And lies on my bed,
She hides at night,
I like to hear her purr,
But one thing I hate about my cat is . . .
She leaves dead mice and birds at my back door,
But I still love her very much!

Emma Moore (9)
Gorran Primary School, Coleraine

The Monster

The monster creaks below the floor,
Waiting until I open the door.
I eventually go to bed,
Then I slightly poke my head
Through the door and,
'Boo!' shouts the monster,
'Aaaarrrggghhh!' I say,
'Who are you?
What are you doing here?
Don't touch me!'

The monster says in a creaky, mean voice,
'I am Triple D.'
'Triple D? What kind of name is that?'
He replied, 'It is a name of evil.'
I shouted, 'Mum, there's someone with a name of evil in the house.'
Mum said, 'Adam, stop annoying your sister.'
The monster said, 'But *Mum!*'

Annabel Steen (8)
Gorran Primary School, Coleraine

Sisters

S isters are cool, they rock!
I t is better to have an older sister because they take you
   everywhere.
S hare secrets with your sisters, but always make a promise
   because if you fall out with her, she will tell your secrets to Mum!
T est your sister to see if she knows her maths.
E ven though they can be just a little bit cross,
R eally my sisters can't get cross with me because they love me
   and I love them,
S o this is why sisters are cool!

Zoe Gibson (9)
Gorran Primary School, Coleraine

My Little Brother

My little brother is such a pain!
He is always playing the PlayStation
And if he's not, he's poking round my stuff.
He is always shouting at me
And he's always playing with my toys when I'm not around.
He always wakes me up in the morning when I am asleep,
Because of that PlayStation or the television.
He is always annoying.
When I am playing with my other brother,
He comes and takes him off me.
I don't know why he wants him
Because he always plays that PlayStation
And when we read a book at night,
It has to be read in his room.
I have to sit at the end of the bed
And he gets to lay in his.
That's why my brother is such a pain!

Jordan Gregg (8)
Gorran Primary School, Coleraine

I Know You've Died

He said to me before he went,
'It's OK, soon you'll be sent.
When I'm gone I'll still be there,
Though you won't see me, I'll still care.
Don't worry about me I am safe,
Only in you, I have faith.'
On my wall there's a photo of you,
When I walk past I think of us two.
We were always together, you never left my side,
But now you're not there, I know you've died.

Charlotte Smith (10)
Haydock English Martyrs RC Primary School, Haydock

Seasons

Here it comes spring again,
With new flowers spreading away.
Then you are here
Now with a newborn deer.

School's over for the summer
No work for six weeks *yeah!*
Have some fun with your friends
This summer will never end *yeah!*

Autumn's here sad and gloomy,
Dark nights will never end
For autumn is back again.

Put your winter clothes on
For winter is here again
Snow will always fall here
Christmas Day will soon be here
Then we start all over again.

Jamie Harrison (10)
Haydock English Martyrs RC Primary School, Haydock

Funny Football

Spoony Rooney on Man U
Stevey Gerrard has bad flu.
When Figo gets badly fouled
He goes off with a nasty scowl.
Chelsea and Man U are the best
And Rafael has a nasty chest.
Rooney likes to dig
With a puffy black wig.
Roy Keane a head like a ball
And Giggs is really, really small!

Adam Forshaw (9)
Haydock English Martyrs RC Primary School, Haydock

The Big Surprise

Soon as I saw it I jumped out of my chair,
Then I gave it a massive stare.
I looked up slowly just to see if it was there,
I opened the top to see what was there.
It was a big soft teddy bear with lots of fur,
I gave it a cuddle with lots of care.

Charlotte Hull (10)
Haydock English Martyrs RC Primary School, Haydock

Holiday

Three days left until it will come
It's so exciting, I am acting really dumb
Two days left, it is almost near,
It is not very far away from here.
The day is here and I'm not acting dumb
I'm really excited, I am glad it has come.

I'm here, I'm here, it is all done,
I'm on my holiday and I'm having fun
I went to the sea and to the pool
And when it was hot the pool was cool.

Luke Pilkington (10)
Haydock English Martyrs RC Primary School, Haydock

My Cool Mum

My mum is cool, she loves me
She sings in the bath while I laugh, hee hee!
When I am tired she tucks me in bed
If I fall off my bike she mends my head.

Callum Jackson (10)
Haydock English Martyrs RC Primary School, Haydock

The Teachers Are Gone

Hip, hip, hooray the teachers are away,
Let's write on the wall and go out to play,
Now we're not sweet, now we're not kind,
Now we don't have to use our minds!

Let's run a riot, let's jump on the chairs,
Let's give our books a good old tear,
Push over the desk, we don't care,
Now we don't call anyone sir!

Beep, beep, beep, the teachers are back
Oh no, they're going to come and attack,
Clean up the room, quick, quick, quick,
The clock is ticking, tick, tick tick!

The doorknob's opening really slow,
Jump through the window, go, go, go
The teacher's face went cherry-red,
'Detention!' I heard as we fled!

Lauren Mason (10)
Haydock English Martyrs RC Primary School, Haydock

Fireworks, Fireworks

Fireworks, fireworks, go and fly
Fireworks, fireworks go up to the sky
Fireworks, fireworks, bright as the sun
Fireworks, fireworks, are such fun.

Fireworks, fireworks bang so loud
Fireworks, fireworks are so proud
Fireworks, fireworks scream so quiet
Fireworks, fireworks are such a riot.

Rece Whitfield ((9)
Haydock English Martyrs RC Primary School, Haydock

Friends That Die

Friends are sad, friends are bad
Friends are happy, friends are sad
You can make them laugh
You can make them cry
But this time it really is goodbye.

You are still here, I can't regret
This time I can't forget
You will always be with me
Every time I walk or stumble
You will always be free.

Stay with me today
And all your troubles will fade away
Make me safe and calm
Help me with my troubles
Keep me safe from harm.

Make me be your friend
Help me to pretend
Don't make me sad
Don't make me bad.

Stay with me forever I know you've died!

Chelsea Smith (10)
Haydock English Martyrs RC Primary School, Haydock

We Don't Obey The Rules

Dance on the table, and have some fun
Go to the staffroom and put ham on the bun.
Steal Miss Lawson's laptop and take it away,
It is time for some games and play.

Go to the staffroom and have a cup of tea,
Then go to the sea in Miss Hannon's car
Uh oh Miss Lawson is on her way back.

Alex Harrison (9)
Haydock English Martyrs RC Primary School, Haydock

My Friend Cares

You may not see me, I'm still there,
Even though you can't see me I'll still care.
Remember when we played together and stayed out late,
I will never forget you, of course you are my best mate.

Together we were the greatest team,
Remember at Hallowe'en we made our neighbours scream!
You were like a brother to me, I was like a sister to you,
I see your house and think of times we went through.

In class we sat next to one another,
Oh you were better than my brother.
I can't wait till I come,
Even though I miss my mum.

I want to be with you,
So once again we become a two.
Now I've got a tear running down,
I know you ask me why I weep and frown.

Lana Kayattiankal (10)
Haydock English Martyrs RC Primary School, Haydock

The Warmth And Cold

I sit raggedly in my chair
I would not move, I would not care.
For what I see outside is a big, cold white cover covering
My slide.

It freezes my fingers
It freezes my toes
But I hate it when you can't feel your nose.

The fire burns in a funny kind of way
The kind that makes you want to sway
The tea tastes deluxe in your throat
Now I just sit and drift away in my big coat.

Thomas Kilgannon (10)
Haydock English Martyrs RC Primary School, Haydock

Now You've Gone

Now you've gone, there's nobody there,
To scamper around and show me some care.
Now night has come, there's no sound at all
And all I want to hear is your call.

Last week I got out of bed,
'Clean your guinea pig,' my mum had said.
But yesterday there was nothing to do,
So I sat up and read.

At night there's nothing in my ear,
Not a crunching, or a munching, nothing to be said.
I sit up, a tear in my eye,
Now I know that you have gone.

Katie Woodward (10)
Haydock English Martyrs RC Primary School, Haydock

School

School is boring when we have to learn,
Set all the books on fire, let them burn.
Have food fights with our lunch,
Let's have a fight, let's all punch.

Now it's our turn to rule the school,
Let's all play a game, this is so cool.
Oh no, the teachers are on their way back,
Just chuck everything in that sack.

Katie Edwards (10)
Haydock English Martyrs RC Primary School, Haydock

Fireworks

Flying through the sky
Right left up down and all around
Like a small rocket.

Then suddenly, *bang, crackle, bang*
Amazing colours,   purple
                      red
                      blue
                      green
                      pink
      lighting up the sky.

You cannot touch them, they're too high,
So don't sigh or even cry.

Jack Day (9)
Haydock English Martyrs RC Primary School, Haydock

Colours

Colours are nice,
Colours are bright
Colours shine in the light.

Colours are cool
Colours are mellow
Colours snort like a little fellow.

Colours are lovely
Colours are puffy
Colours are snuggly!

Chloe Dowd (10)
Haydock English Martyrs RC Primary School, Haydock

The Bug Chant

Yellow bugs, mellow bugs,
Lazy little fellow bugs.

Green bugs, unseen bugs,
Lanky, long and lean bugs.

Thin bugs, fat bugs,
Find them in your hat bugs.

Black bugs, tack bugs,
Always get the sack bugs.

Happy bugs, grumpy bugs,
Behaving like a monkey bugs.

Red bugs, bed bugs,
Find them in your head bugs.

Pink bugs, think bugs,
Swimming in your drink bugs.

Boy bugs, girl bugs,
Lots of smelly, hairy bugs!

Jacob Adair (10)
Haydock English Martyrs RC Primary School, Haydock

Rugby Mad

The rugby kicked off and the whistle was blown
As the ball came down, they got out their phone.

The crowd sang, 'Rugby crazy, rugby mad
Come on Saints, be bad, bad, bad.'

At half-time the crowd all cheered,
And there were four men with dirty beers.

Connor Hewitt (10)
Haydock English Martyrs RC Primary School, Haydock

My Family

I have a strange family,
I do try to complain,
But they always laugh at me,
Now let me explain.

I have an older sister,
She's obsessed with all the boys!
And then there is the younger one,
She makes a heck of a noise!

Sitting in her high chair,
Throwing around her food,
Talking with her mouth full,
Oh, she's just so rude!

All he does is pick his nose,
That is my twin brother!
But I haven't finished yet, at all,
What about my mother?

Yes, she does the washing and ironing,
And cooks all of our food,
But when it comes to housework,
She does it in the nude!

My dad thinks he's so, so cool,
Cos he used to be in the navy,
But since he left to be with us
He's gone completely sport crazy.

That just then leaves me,
The only normal one,
But I guess if we were all the same
There would never be any fun!

Sophie Allisett (11)
Hillbourne Middle School, Poole

Why?

Why does the sun stay in the sky?
Why are the clouds always so high?
Why do birds fly in the sky?

Please can someone tell me *why!*

Why does the sun stay in the sky?
Why are we born?
And why do we die?

Please can someone tell me *why!*

Why does the sun stay in the sky?
Why do we go to school?
Why do we have to follow rules?

Please can someone tell me *why!*

Why does the sun stay in the sky?
Why do we laugh -
When others cry?
Please can someone tell me *why!*

Somebody *please* tell me why, why, *why!*

Katie Sneddon (9)
Hillbourne Middle School, Poole

Poole

Poole is big
Full of things to do
Swim at the seaside
Or at the indoor pool
Shopping in the high street
Chips on the quay
Everybody knows
Poole is the place to be.

Charlie Jones (9)
Hillbourne Middle School, Poole

Christmas Day

C hristms Day is a time for joy
H ear a child playing with their toy
R eindeer are on the rooftop
I see mums shop till they drop
S now is falling anywhere and everywhere
T ime for Christmas, my brother doesn't care
M y friends are all playing in the snow
A my doesn't know where in the snow to go
S anta's here, I want to see him, Mum said no.

D aniel is excitedly counting down for Christmas Day
A friend of mine on Christmas Day is going away
Y es I've finished my poem, now I've found out it's May!

Sarah Benfield (11)
Hillbourne Middle School, Poole

Water Aid

Water, water is the miracle of life.
Water, fresh water will keep you alive,
No clean water will kill many lives,
Africa and Asia are countries that are poor,
Water aid will help them for sure.
Disease, starvation, dehydration,
The little children suffer with no sanitation.
So please, please help the people who suffer, so
Boys and girls like us will never have to suffer.

Charlie Bishop (8)
Hillbourne Middle School, Poole

Teeth

Teeth, teeth
They chew on chewy beef
They sometimes go yellow
So you must brush your teeth!

Teeth, teeth
They rip apart beef
And meat that humans eat
They sometimes go yellow
So you must brush your teeth!

Aimee Auger (10)
Hillbourne Middle School, Poole

Why?

Why is the sky so high?
Why are the clouds so high?

Why do we have brothers and sisters?
Why do we fight each other?

Why do we need money?

Why do we need to pay so much
Money now?

Why do we need to kill people and animals?

Christine Lovell (10)
Hillbourne Middle School, Poole

Shoes!

I've got shoes, black and white,
Some that give me an awful fright,
Some that are red as roses,
Some that do awful poses,
Some that like to whisper,
Some that have got pairs of brothers and sisters,
Some smell like awful cheese,
Some like to also tease,
Small ones, big ones, one's baby sized,
They're all going to win the weirdest shoes prize.

Ella Brooks (10)
Hillbourne Middle School, Poole

The Way I See It!

The moving object rocks to and fro,
And all the lights are really low,
The lightning strikes upon the house,
And as the house has a louse

It makes it seem alive,
As the creature dives,
He makes so many eerie shadows,
It really frightens me.

I shout for help,
But nobody listens to me,
For I'm a ghost!

Jessica Wiffin (10)

How Do You Act?

How do you act when your parents are around?
Shouting and bawling or
A quiet little angel not making a sound?

What do you do when your mum tells you off?
Fall to the ground kicking and crying
Or go and be sweet to good old Daddy?

Where do you go after an argument?
Go out and slam the door
Or run quickly up to your bed and sob.

How do you react when your dad goes away for 2 weeks?
Are you holding your head up high
Or are you *hitting* everything in reach?

Alice Higgins (11)
Holystone Primary School, Newcastle upon Tyne

Night

When it is night,
I can sometimes get a fright,
As I can hear a funny noise,
And wonder, *could it be my toys?*

So I listen and keep still,
But normally it's my supermarket till,
My eyes glare,
And think, get out of bed or should I dare?

But then my doll starts coughing,
I realise it's nothing,
My head hits the pillow,
And I fall asleep with my teddy, Willow.

Brooke Foster (10)
Holystone Primary School, Newcastle upon Tyne

It's Serious

Calling 999 is serious,
It is not a game to play,
It could cause a lot of problems,
When done in the wrong way.

The firemen could be saving lives,
Instead of receiving tricks,
They could be putting out fires,
And getting there quick.

There are not enough fire engines,
To take hoax calls,
It wastes time to save people,
With fires in their halls.

Juliette Amers (10)
Holystone Primary School, Newcastle upon Tyne

The Castle

She watches you up in the sky
Her eyes glittering
Her smile so big
But then she starts to open the gate
She spooks me out a lot!

She waits till after school for *me!*
I'm not scared
No!
Argh! Oh no she's
Gobbled me up.

Rosie Duerdin (10)
Holystone Primary School, Newcastle upon Tyne

The Runaway

Once upon a time
I caught a little rhyme

I set it on the floor
It ran straight out the door.

I chased it on my bicycle
It melted to an icicle.

I scooped it in my hat
It turned into a rat.

I caught it by the tail
It stretched into a whale.

I followed it in a boat,
It changed into a goat.

When I fed it tin and paper
It became a tall skyscraper.

Then it grew into a kite
And flew far out of my sight.

Kayleigh Leung (9)
Holystone Primary School, Newcastle upon Tyne

Frightened?

Shadows dancing, prancing about
They're coming to get you, there's no doubt,
Lurking, jerking, smirking, you're the one,
That they're going to leap upon.

You're heading for your death,
Nothing but your brittle bones will be left,
Scared are you?
You'd better be too!

Lauren Scollins (10)
Holystone Primary School, Newcastle upon Tyne

Seasons

Spring is the blossoming season of the year,
Easter bunnies, chocolate eggs and fields of daffodils everywhere
The sound of birds whistling is a delight,
Bright early mornings,
Late evenings and nights.

Summer is the season we all look forward to,
Six week break, no work, no school,
You can fly abroad,
You can stay at home,
As long as a good time is had by all.

Autumn is a signal
The cold is on its way,
Woolly hat, scarves and gloves are the order of the day,
Leaves fall from the trees,
Plants wither and fade away.

Winter is here,
It's Christmas time again,
Giving and receiving presents,
Lots to eat and lots to do,
And if we're really lucky it may snow too!

Cherelle Whyte (9)
Horsenden Primary School, Greenford

Djibril Cisse

He's a shooting rock star
He's a speeding jaguar
He's a firework cracking
A star flying through the sky
The loud instrument playing.

The bullet scurrying around
A flying rocket.

Yasir Khan
Horsenden Primary School, Greenford

The Bonfire Night

It is Bonfire Night
The sky is so bright
Fireworks go crack, bang,
'Wow,' says a gang.

Fireworks are so fabulous; well that is how I see
Because they are so beautiful, I wish they were me.
Everyone in the city gathers round in the night
Very little children cover their ears very tight.

Fireworks are good
They bang as they should
The little children have the fright
Their faces have gone pale and white

So now you know all about Bonfire Night
Plus all the children who have the fright
You know the fireworks are good
You be safe as you should.

Ritu Elaswarapu (9)
Horsenden Primary School, Greenford

Wayne Rooney

He's as fast as a cheetah.
He's ten buildings put together.
He's a door always closed and you need a key to open it.
He's a massive bank.

He's a shooting star.
He's a wave always on the move.
He's a flying plane.
He's got dragon's pain.

He's the king of goddesses.
He's as clever as a dolphin.
He's got the balance of a cat.
He's a sparkling morning with a sharp shower.

Saawan Parekh (9)
Horsenden Primary School, Greenford

Babies

Crawling around the house
Like a little mouse
They are quite cheeky
They are also sneaky
They can crawl around
Without making any sound
So without any doubt
Watch out!

Gliding on the floors
In and out of doors
Playing on the table
Though they are unstable
Scattering their toys
Making lots of noise,
So without any doubt
Watch out!

Always, always smashing
Followed by some crashing
Eating off the rug
Like a little bug
They like to be fed
But hate going to bed
So without any doubt
Watch out!

Never being neat
Playing with their feet
Even though they are naughty
We love them very much
So without any doubt
Watch out!

Shehan Dasan (9)
Horsenden Primary School, Greenford

A Is For . . .

A is for angry, agile anacondas.
B is for bright, beautiful butterflies.
C is for crafty, cunning crocodiles.
D is for dodging, daring dingoes.
E is for elegant, energetic elephants.
F is for furry, friendly felines,
G is for grand, graceful giraffes.
H is for happy, hungry hippos.
I is for itchy, inventive insects.
J is for jumping, jogging jaguars.
K is for kind, keen koalas.
L is for loud, lazy lions.
M is for mad, mischievous monkeys.
N is for nifty, naughty newts.
O is for odd, oceanic octopuses.
P is for pretty, pink panthers.
Q is for quaint, quirky quails.
R is for roaming, rambling rabbits.
S is for sly, slithering snakes.
T is for tough, terrifying tigers.
U is for unique, unknown unicorns.
V is for vicious, vigilant vampires.
W is for wet, wiggly worms.
X is for xxx . . . not in our world.
Y is for yapping, yelling yaks.
Z is for zippy, zany zebras.

Jemma Laird (9)
Horsenden Primary School, Greenford

My Sister

I remember the day my sister was born
It was a cold, windy night
I had to go to my friend's house
When I came home I was so excited
I cuddled her and kissed her
I called her Apricot
She called me Diddy
I just love my sister!

She grew up very quickly
Soon she started annoying me
And we would kick and fight
I hate it as she doesn't get told off
She gets away with everything
And I'm left with bruises and the blame
I just hate my sister!

One day my sister went away
I thought it would be great
But I missed her
I had nobody to argue with
Or mess around with
I cried
When she came back I was so happy
I just love and hate my sister!

Elizabeth Appleby (9)
Horsenden Primary School, Greenford

My Class

I am in Year 5
I go to Horsenden School
My teacher is Mr Joahill
And his class is always cool.

There are thirty-one children
All wonderful girls and boys
We listen to Mr Joahill
And don't make a lot of noise.

The subjects he teaches us
Are science, history, literacy
ICT, DT, PE, art,
And my favourite subject - numeracy.

My friends from 5H
Are the best I've ever had
We help each other
And none of us are bad.

Dushan Despotovic (9)
Horsenden Primary School, Greenford

Riddle

It has no beginning
It has no end,
It is used at a wedding
It is a promise of love.

It is found on a car
Or a bike or a plane,
In a nose of a pig
Or a nose of a bull.

It is used as a plaything
Or to wear in your ear,
It can be diamonds or rubies
It's a wonderful ring.

Bhavethaa Barathithasan (10)
Horsenden Primary School, Greenford

My Friend

I like the way you make me smile.
I like the way you make me laugh.
I like the way you make me sing.
I like the way you make me dance.

I like it when you laugh at my jokes.
I like it when you play with my toys.
I like it when you dance to my music.
I like it when you sing to my songs.

I like you because you're kind.
I like you because you're cool.
I like you because you're funny.
I like you because you're my friend.

I like your eyes.
I like your hair.
I like your clothes.
I like the way you care.

I like:
Your smile,
Your laugh,
Your personality,
Which makes me grin.

I like the way you laugh at me.
I like the way you grin at me.
I like the way you respect me.
I like the way you treat me.

I like all these things about you.
You make me happy with your grin.
You respect me,
That is why I respect you.

Anuthya Nambirajah (9)
Horsenden Primary School, Greenford

Christmas Time

Trees are glittering and decorated
With tinsel and balls.
Phones constantly ringing with cheerful
Christmas calls.
Presents piled up as high as Santa flies
Rudolph jingling bells, ringing across the skies
Families getting together, children playing
All night long.

Carollers sweetly singing a joyful Christmas song.
Hot Christmas dinner, friendly table chat.
Popping Christmas crackers filled with paper hats.
Mistletoe and holly decorated across the walls
Gifts of all sizes, long, short or tall.
Happy Christmas spirit that is happening every minute,
Dancing and celebrating throughout the night.
Dazzling Christmas lights shining all so bright
When Christmas is over, don't you fear!
We can cherish this day every year.

Aneesha Bhumber (10)
Horsenden Primary School, Greenford

The Brain

We all have brains,
Big and small.
It tells us when it hurts when we fall!
We use our brain for thinking and feeling
It also helps us with the cleaning!
The brain has two sides, left and right
It sends messages for our sight
The left side helps us with reading and writing
The right side helps with pictures and rhyming.
When we're upset the brain sends signals
And we start crying.
It also knows when you are lying!

Bethany Marshall (9)
Horsenden Primary School, Greenford

About My Personal Life

I know this guy called Eddy
He is sporty and is fun
And can crack funny jokes
And he can surely run

He goes to Horsenden Primary School
To learn and play
He has a teacher called Mrs Collins
Who teaches him every day

He has many many friends
Who go to his school
They mess about
And have fun in the pool.

He is into PlayStation
Goes on it every day
Gets 'Games Weekly'
And never stops to play.

Then the week starts again
Time to go to school
Walks down Whitton Avenue
By following the school rules.

Edward Nana-Ansah
Horsenden Primary School, Greenford

My Chocolatey Poem

Chocolate, chocolates, chocolatey brown
Take off any type of frown.
Chocolate, chocolate very yummy
A perfect meal for my tummy
White, brown or black,
It's still a tasty snack!

Rianne Shiebak
Horsenden Primary School, Greenford

Fantasy Land

Fantasy Land is an island with beautiful flowers,
With high mountains as tall as brick towers,
The grass is green and the trees strong,
And the birds sing a marvellous song,
It is a happy land, Fantasy Land, though it is rather small.

It is a land, so far away,
Where it's bright and peaceful all day,
And all the birds come out and say,
'Go to Fantasy Land for a holiday.'

The pixies and fairies have pretty long hair,
The angels have halos and are rather fair,
The animals and creatures that live around,
Know it's lovely and quiet, there isn't a sound.

The shimmering sun and azure sky,
The rainbow floating, way up high,
And down below, we all know that it's Fantasy Land
We can only dream of.

Charlene De Alwis (9)
Horsenden Primary School, Greenford

Frank Lampard

He is a star shooter
He is a great person
He is a great footballer
A wicked footballer
He is the best footballer
He smells like a hardworking man
He is the greatest man!

Vinay Vaghijani (9)
Horsenden Primary School, Greenford

Dragons

Dragons breathe fire,
Dragons breathe ice,
Dragons steal treasure,
Dragons live forever.

Dragons fly high
Like clouds in the sky.
Dragons take pride in the way they fly
Dragons' wing beats are big gusts of wind
Dragons have dreams of becoming all mean.

Dragons' hearts are shared with men
Who believe in them
Dragons live in lands long forgotten
And not foretold.

Dragons have the wisdom
Of a thousand wise men
But for some of them it is their end.

Christian Gonzalez (9)
Horsenden Primary School, Greenford

My Flower

I saw a flower,
It made me smile.
I saw a flower,
Standing out in the rain.
I saw a flower,
Covered in snow.
I saw a flower,
Slowly opening its petals
Towards the sun.

Shabri Mehta (9)
Horsenden Primary School, Greenford

My Mum

She's as bright as the sun,
She's a fast shooting star
She's a cool dog,
The smell of fully grown roses.
The nicest fairy godmother,
A lucky person.
She's a funny person,
She's a cool mum.
She's the best cooker alive,
She's a fire-breathing dragon.
A swan all proud,
She's a soft bear,
A puff of silver,
She's a waterslide,
A wave when crashing,
A calm fish.

Anitta Sritharan (9)
Horsenden Primary School, Greenford

A Cat

Eyes of evil dark
Teeth of devil shark
Witch's lucky pet
But everyone's best
Some are dead-black
Some are snow-white
But either way, they are all a cute sight.
Some are fluffy
Some are rough
But a great friend to make your life happy
Their great stare makes you care.

Tharsika Muralitharan (10)
Horsenden Primary School, Greenford

Summer's Day

Everyone comes out to play on a
Lovely English summer's day,
Get dressed first,
Have breakfast,
And take our balls and bats,
Everyone comes out to play on
A lovely English summer's day.
We run away,
Talk all day,
And play as much as we can,
Everyone comes out to play on a
Lovely English summer's day,
It's the best,
It beats the rest,
That lovely English summer's day!

Louisa Stivaros (10)
Horsenden Primary School, Greenford

Twist Me And Lick Me

Twist me and lick me
Turn me around

Eat me and drink me
Put me down

Pull me and push me
Flip me upside down

Kiss me and swish me
Twirl me about.

Wet me and dry me
Curl me round your finger

Can you guess what I am?

Fatema Sulemanji (10)
Horsenden Primary School, Greenford

My Trip To School

Wake up at seven o'clock
Mum comes in *knock, knock, knock*
Put on my uniform
Do my hair
Sister's asleep, that's not fair.

Go to the bathroom
Brush my teeth
Look for my toothbrush
Where could it be?
Look in the cupboards
Look in the drawers
Guess what? It's under the floorboards.

Go downstairs, have a cup of tea
I look out the window, what do I see?
Oh dear! Mum's been attacked by a bee.
Mum comes in, shuts the door
Shouting and screaming
Stamping the floor.

Off we go or we'll be late
We don't want them to shut the gate.
Hooray! I'm here
I have no fear
Get in my line
I'm right on time!

Laura Youna (10)
Horsenden Primary School, Greenford

Charlie And The Chocolate Factory

'Daddy I want this
Daddy I want that,'
Verruca would always say,
'Now Daddy, I want a squirrel and a golden goose,'
And he would always say, 'OK.'

Now Mike TV is crazy
Always complaining about his food
He is always watching TV
Being all lazy, and moaning to his parents
Not like he should be.

Chew, chew, chew
Is what Violet would always do
Trying to beat her friend
She blew up and still she'd chew.

Augustus Gloop was fat
He was always eating
His heart was hardly beating
Because he was sooooooo unhealthy!

Charlie was a poor child
Very kind and friendly
Then he won the chocolate factory
And was rich and happy!

Mona Jamil (10)
Horsenden Primary School, Greenford

Ocean View

The sea can be calm or violent.
It can be a friend or a foe.
The sea shimmers in the moonlight and shines brightly in the sun.
It can swallow up most things like a black hole
But also help us travel the globe.
It shines many different colours, in fact all the colours of the rainbow.
It eats up ships and is very dangerous, yet it also helps us too.
Without the sea there would be no fish and where would we also be.

Next to the sea lies the beach
And on the beach lie people, shells and a lot of sand.
The shells are spiky, smooth or rough.
There are different colours and sizes of shells.
The people on the beach are short, tall, skinny or fat.
They are also different colours.

Avinash Bakshi (9)
Horsenden Primary School, Greenford

Merry Christmas

M ellowing mice murmur melodies
E ating elephants ignore elegance
R evolting records recognise rhymes
R oaring red rabbits ride on rainbows
Y awning yellow yellers yell

C hristmas carols call curiously
H ats hatter hating headaches
R attling rangers race rain
I cy igloos invent icy ideas
S now slithering softly
T ickling tigers tangle tails
M aroon marshmallows in marmalade
A ccounting animals add acting actors
S enior singers sail simply.

Radhika Bathia (9)
Horsenden Primary School, Greenford

A Sailing Boat

I saw a ship a-sailing,
A-sailing on the sea,
And it was deeply laden
With pretty things for me.

There were raisins in the cabin,
And almonds in the hold;
The sails were made of silk,
And the masts were all of gold.

The four-and-twenty sailors,
That stood between the decks,
Were four-and-twenty white mice
With chains about their necks.

The captain was a duck
With a jacket on his back,
And when the ship began to move
The captain said, 'Quack! Quack!'

Aaron Eni
Horsenden Primary School, Greenford

Chocolate!

Chocolate is the best treat,
They sell it on every high street.

There's different types - such as white,
But it makes your clothes very tight.

A different chocolate colour is brown,
If you eat too much your tummy will frown.

The last type is black,
But if you eat too much, you'll get a *smack!*

Sharihaan Ahmad (9)
Horsenden Primary School, Greenford

Loving You

I'm young
Yet I feel old
But you are so beautiful
Beautiful as gold.

I love you with all my heart
With all the love for you
Do you love me?
'Cause I love you

You are my world
You make my day
I make sculptures of you with clay.

I love you
I'll love you till the day I die
Until I go to Heaven
Way up high.

Sumiyya Iqbal (9)
Horsenden Primary School, Greenford

Waterfall

Cold, sparkling water in a rush
Carrying the littered leaves
Fallen from the trees,
With bundles of sticks
And once laying logs.
Splash! Gush! Whoosh!
Goes the leaves like a one-way racing track,
Once you fall in, there is no hope to save.
At the bottom all is calm and silent
Not like the fall itself where it is noisy and violent.
The churning of the water, everything is white and misty
Until the water gleams and shines
At the end of the waterfall
Everything is fine.

Hana Jali (9)
Horsenden Primary School, Greenford

My School Years

Horsenden Primary School,
How it is all so cool,
From reception to Year 5,
I have merrily survived.

Mrs Mason for reception,
I gave her all my attention,
She may be very strict,
But for a teacher this is fit.

Mrs Little and Mrs Gribbon,
Were never stern,
They took me for Year 1,
They're teachers to everyone.

Oh dear Mr Moseley,
He was so funny!
I had him for Year 2,
He could draw funny pictures too.

Miss Rout, who became Mrs Troughton,
Left when she was pregnant,
Later came Miss Crawley,
A replacement for Year 3.

Year 4 with Mrs Lobo,
She has a son named Rio,
She loved playing games,
Games that were never lame.

Mrs Wesley who is small,
Miss Collins who is tall,
My teachers for Year 5,
I am having a fantastic life!

Angela Lam (10)
Horsenden Primary School, Greenford

What's Freaky?

Whilst walking along
I found this key
I knocked on the door
And along came he.

Along he came
To the door to see
This terrified boy
Who was me

'Please Sir,' I said
Holding out the key
'I think this is yours
Maybe.'

'Thank you,' he said
His eyes full of glee
'Why don't you come in
And have some tea.'

'No thanks,' I said
'I'd rather have a fee,'
'Five pounds,' he said
'No fifty!'

'Fifty!' he said
'Do you think I'm silly?
Have you met my big dog?
His name is . . . *Bonecrusher!*'

Now that's a free-key story.

Kush Bhandari (9)
Horsenden Primary School, Greenford

Friends Forever

Friends are kind and thoughtful
Who you can always trust,
That's why we have best friends
It's a certain must.

A friend is always there
To support you all the time
You can always rely on them,
Even if they drink cherry lime.

When you give out invitations
They never ever say no.
If you're really kind to them
Then they won't have to go.

A friend is like a shining star
As bright as can be
No matter what she'll be there
And will never leave me.

Me and my friend
Always have a lot of fun
We always play together
In the shining sun.

Best friends always stick together
When there are ups and downs
Best friends never leave each other
Even when they're in different towns.

Tayyaba Ahmad (9)
Horsenden Primary School, Greenford

My Pet

I have an exotic pet
Who's fierce but also cute,
But there's something I don't get
He goes *miaow* and *hoot hoot*

His body is yellow and green
With black eyes on his head,
For fun I call him Dean
His face is bright red.

We play a lot of games
They are really great,
I sometimes call him names
Like my best friend and my mate.

To name his species you'll never guess
You will never spoil my plot,
He really is the best
He's a large African parrot.

Luke Campbell (9)
Horsenden Primary School, Greenford

Apple

It is as soft as a baby's cheek
I eat some every week.
It is as sweet as honey,
And costs very little money.

It is as colourful as a party balloon,
And round like a full moon.
It is very crunchy,
And gives me lots of energy.

It can be the colours of a traffic light
And it is all shiny and bright.
When I eat my apple pie,
I say to hunger goodbye.

Khaled Abdellatiff (9)
Horsenden Primary School, Greenford

Hallowe'en

Beware it's Hallowe'en
There are zombies that are green.
Beware sour limes that
Turn into green slime.

Beware, a mouse turns
Into a haunted house.
Beware vampires suck your blood,
And leave a blood flood.

Beware you're in for a scare
A scare that will take out all your hair.
Beware witches take out your brains,
And use them for haunted trains.

Beware wolves will kill your cat
And turn it into your bedroom mat.
Beware the skeleton is back,
He'll put your head in a sack.

Beware Frankenstein is here
He'll take off both your ears.
Beware of the haunted bat,
It will turn you very fat.

Maryam Bux (9)
Horsenden Primary School, Greenford

Ice Rocket

I have a deliciously tropical taste,
I am very sweet and juicy,
I make you shiver when you eat me,
And make your hands extremely sticky.
If you leave me too long in the sun,
I'll melt before you can eat me.

Chloe Charles (9)
Horsenden Primary School, Greenford

The Angry Alligators

The angry alligators are Amy's apple!
Then the bouncy bears baked some bread!
The crazy cat was climbing a chimney!
The dangerous dog was doing some dog drama!
Elegant elephants were eating eggs!
The funny frogs went to the fiesta!
Girly giraffe got the gold!
Helpful hare hugged hopeless hippotamus!
Icy igloo had irritating insects!
Circus Jack juggled jugs of juice!
Keen kangaroo kicked kind cat!
Loopy lion licked lots of lollipops!
Mean monkeys mugged most of the money!
Naughty nits nicked the nuts!
Old octopus peeled an orange!
Pretty parrot ate the prawns!
Cute queen quarrelled a lot!
Ruby rabbit rowed the boat!
Slithery snake saw the strawberries!
Two tigers taught how to play tag!
Unlucky otters had an umbrella!
The vampires smashed the vase!
Watery whales washed the wings!
Scary x-rays aren't good!
My yard had yummy food!
Stripy zebra has a zipped jacket!
Angels arranged a line of apples!
Brilliant boys bounced a ball!
Creamy cake tasted good!
Dreamy dodo had a dog!

Neeki Doroudian (9)
Horsenden Primary School, Greenford

The Eerie Castle

On a walk through the woods one day
I saw a vision dark and grey.
On the other side of the lake,
Stood a castle, eerie and desolate.

It loomed at the edge of the wood,
And I stopped still where I stood.
My heart was pounding loud and clear,
Was it surprise, awe or fear!

The house seemed to beckon me in,
To unravel the secrets within.
The overgrown weeds, the ivy on the walls,
The sullen windows, the turrets tall.

They all seemed to have a story to tell,
Was it a gate to Heaven or a pathway to Hell?
I crept closer for a better view,
Treading on grass laden with dew.

The knocker was heavy and rusty too.
And echoed loudly the whole house through.
The hinges creaked, the door opened wide,
A tiny step and I was inside.

Silken webs and spiders galore,
Creaky boards where I walked on the floor.
An open fireplace and windows tall,
A spiral staircase rising from the great hall.

I wandered there from room to room,
But there was nothing but darkness and gloom.
No laughter, no joy, or any cheer,
Just deep sadness which was very clear.

I shall never know the secrets there,
The burden that the house must bear.

Nidhi Sunderam (10)
Horsenden Primary School, Greenford

Lions

Lions are funny
Lions are smooth
Lions have magnificent manes
Lions are dangerous
Lions are ferocious
Lions are fast and this is true
Lions are loud
Lions are large
Lions are fierce like anything else
Lions are strong
Lions are frightening more than anything else
Lions are cuddly
Lions are soft
A female lion is called a lioness
Lions are furious
Lions are mad
Lions have cubs that can be so playful at times.

Roshni Rabheru (9)
Horsenden Primary School, Greenford

The Sea

It's cold as a snowman.
It's whale bashing.
It's a shining crystal.
It's an aeroplane crashing.

It's as thin as a pencil.
It's as cold as ice.
It's fast as a cheetah.
It's quick as mice.

It sways together, it's lovely.
It's bright as a star.
It shines beautifully,
It's my magical star.

Zoya Hussain (10)
Horsenden Primary School, Greenford

The Sky From My Window

I looked out
Of my window last night
And saw a full moon.
It was shaped like a circle.
The colour of the moon was pure-white
Like a piece of paper.
First it looked a bit like a banana
But then it grew into a full moon.

In the morning I looked outside my window
And I saw a lovely blue sky
With a lot of clouds
Which I thought looked
A bit like candyfloss.
I thought about how amazing it was
And how the sky changes.

Stephen Danes (9)
Horsenden Primary School, Greenford

Life

Life is like a video game,
Very challenging but always has to end.
You start at the beginning, a baby,
Crying constantly through the night.
Then a child, running freely in the gentle breeze,
With friends altogether playing noisily.
Now an adult, mature and sensible
Working responsibly until dark.
The elderly, laugh happily
Showing off their new set of teeth
Before saying goodbye.

Dina Morsy-Fahmy (9)
Horsenden Primary School, Greenford

My Front Door

See
Going through my front door
I can see
A shiny new piano
My stairs
Cream *everywhere*
Cream carpet
Cream tiles
Cream lights!

Hear
Going through my front door
I can hear
The washing machine
Going round and round
Bart Simpson
Talking on the TV
Music in the background.

Smell
Going through my front door
I can smell
Friesias from the bathroom
Lemon air fresheners
Stew from the kitchen.

Feel
Going through my front door
I feel
Warm
Comfortable
Ready to relax in front of the TV.

James Walton (9)
Horsenden Primary School, Greenford

My Dog

He's a bouncy ball
He's a spiky hedgehog
He's a racing car
He's a lazy beast.

He's a fierce lion
He's a cuddly bear
He's a silver moon
He's a spooky Dracula.

He's a smelly pig
He's a funny clown
He's an angel's pet
He's a bouncy kangaroo.

Laylan Siddik (9)
Horsenden Primary School, Greenford

Steven Gerrard

He's a fast cheetah
He's a king who's so fast
He's a speedy Ferrari
He's a god on grass.

He's a powerful bullet
He's a dream
He's a magician at work
He's a player in a team.

He's a whiz on the pitch
He's a shining star
He's a good chef in the kitchen
He's my hero Steven Gerrard.

Dean Boothe (9)
Horsenden Primary School, Greenford

Sun

It's a volcano spreading lava
It's the Devil's home
It's the light above my head
It's a dome.

It's a sparkling crystal
It's a baseball
It's a round football
It's an eyeball.

It's a ninja weapon
It's a fireball in outer space
It's an orange egg
It's an orange face.

Hashim Hussain (9)
Horsenden Primary School, Greenford

My Little Sister

She's sweet as a rose
And wet as a hose.
She's cheeky as a monkey
And annoying like a donkey.

She's cute as a cat
And lies on a mat.
She's clever and
Soft as a feather.

She's nice and
Hates mice
She's always behind
But has a great mind.

Sara Tofiq   (9)
Horsenden Primary School, Greenford

Football

My favourite thing is football
My best player is Dan Shittu
Dan Shittu simply is the best
As he makes it four-two.

He plays for Queens Park Rangers
Wearing blue and white hoops
He must be the best player
With his right foot he makes fantastic scoops.

Paul Furlong now has the ball
He makes a fantastic pass
The ball nearly goes to the keeper
But Dan scores by sliding along the grass.

Have you ever seen such a player
With all that skill
The way he controls the ball
I think he's just brill.

The way he runs down the pitch
At just the right speed
He scores yet another goal
That's just what we need.

He's running down the pitch again
Then blasts the ball into the net
That makes his seventh goal
The match isn't over yet.

When the final whistle blows
The crowd give a mighty cheer
They have won seven-two
Then in the bar they'll have a beer.

Daniel Cox (9)
Horsenden Primary School, Greenford

My Mum

My mum is a general.
She stalks through the house
Telling me what to do.
She then sleeps throughout the night
But when she wakes up . . .
Her medals clanking, stars shining
And roars us to attention.
She barks orders as she charges
Throughout the house.
'Naim, do the dishes!
'Naim, clean your room!'
Then crawls back to her bedroom
While we her dutiful slaves
Carry out her orders.

Naim Rahim
Horsenden Primary School, Greenford

Fear

As I walk on my own
Fear pounces on me like a tiger
Waiting to feed on its prey.
The whole world turns against me
And makes me dizzy
I feel so isolated
Like a big black creature
It hovers over me making my vision of life
Just disappear
It comes closer and closer
Opening its mouth ready to
Feed on my happy feelings
Until I am left with my darkest experiences and memories.

Maariyah Esat (11)
Lammack Primary School, Blackburn

Love

He broke up with me,
He first got down on his knee,
Then he said it,
He scared me a bit,
My heart is now broken,
Why does love have to hurt?

Love and hurt takes over me,
Like a massive bee,
Stinging my heart,
Now we will always be apart,
My heart is now broken,
Why does love have to hurt?

The feeling is overpowering me,
It walks slowly around me,
Love makes my heart flutter,
It feels so unnatural,
Like a person walking all over me,
Why does love have to hurt?

Charlotte Jackson (10)
Lammack Primary School, Blackburn

Fear

Fear is a dark shadow following you.
It doesn't touch you but you still feel it.
And when you hear a twig break, it sends
                    shivers down your spine.
Then you feel the eerie chill which makes your hair
                    stand on end.
But the sound, the sound that makes you run and hide,
is the knife.

Thomas Johnson (10)
Lammack Primary School, Blackburn

Fear

Fear is something I am scared of
It sometimes makes me scream.
The fear runs up my back and then
Spreads like a disease.
I can feel it coming towards me,
As it crawls up to me
And all I can do is;
Scream, scream and *scream.*

Zahra Bahadur (11)
Lammack Primary School, Blackburn

Fear

The two figures that creep up behind me
Haunting me like a pair of ghosts
Fear creeping up and down my back
Taking over me scarily.

Ayesha Ougradar (11)
Lammack Primary School, Blackburn

Fear

My colour is fading,
My lips are dry,
My heart is thumping,
Oh why, oh why.
The Death Eaters are coming,
To take me away,
And blackbirds are humming,
Whilst they sway and sway.
Fear has taken over,
It follows me around,
Oh, how I wish on a clover
So that I could never be found.

Mehreen Shah (11)
Lammack Primary School, Blackburn

Sadness!

So sad,
Lost in a world of nothingness,
My soul is far away,
I want to move but have no legs,
The feeling is taking over my body,
I can't breathe.

Heather Mashiter (10)
Lammack Primary School, Blackburn

Loneliness

It creeps towards me,
Wrapping its body around mine.
Taking me to another place,
Another world,
Not letting me move,
Keeping me in my dark corner.
In a dark place,
Loneliness
Just follows me around.

Aamirah Hasan (10)
Lammack Primary School, Blackburn

Fear

The feeling of fear takes over me
It feels like fear pushed me into a dark hole
And I can't get out.
Fear looks like a dark, tall shadow
Lying down in the grass.
Waiting for you to come to it,
Waiting for you all night!

Linzi Robertson (10)
Lammack Primary School, Blackburn

Jealousy

Jealousy is a cold-hearted figure
With a million sharp teeth,
His breath is as smelly
As unwashed feet.

He swallows me up
Into a world of dark,
I fill up with guilt
It leaves a stinging mark.

I try to escape
His unwanted land,
But he grabs me back,
In his firm, wrinkled hand.

Grace Handscomb (10)
Lammack Primary School, Blackburn

Lonely

As his icy mouth sucks out your soul, with his pure evil mind racing.
Leaving me with nothing, no one, only me, myself and I.
Then, with his piercing eerie voice, he laughs a shrill laugh.
He glides away with my soul as I watch with sorrow.
His horrifying eyes, staring straight at me, with hatred and disgust!
He now wanders in my mind, his shrill and terrifying voice,
                                                    still in my head.
I have no one to turn to. No friends.
Loneliness wells up inside me, I can't overcome it.

Loneliness is my fear, nightmare and . . . life!

Kasongo Swana (10)
Lammack Primary School, Blackburn

Fear

Fear is following me
It is wherever I go
When I run it runs
I am lost in an empty cave.

I feel like a wasp is coming to sting me,
Or a man is coming to kidnap me.
Fear is here,
Wherever I go.

A tiger pounces,
You run and hide,
But fear is near,
Wherever you are!

Amelia Dunning (10)
Lammack Primary School, Blackburn

Fear

He keeps you awake at night,
He is always ready to give you a fright,
The monster crawling up your back,
Waiting until his time to attack.

His shadow hangs over you,
Blocking out the moonlight,
His deep voice echoes inside your head,
He says . . .

    'You won't sleep tonight.'

Fern Nicholas (11)
Lammack Primary School, Blackburn

Love

The second he told me the world began to spin.
The bright light of love began to dim.
He said he hated me from the start,
Those very words broke my heart.
I told him:
Love is a warm feeling in my tummy
When it's taken away, my throat goes dry.
I feel like I've been stabbed by a thousand knives.

Sophie Jones (10)
Lammack Primary School, Blackburn

Loneliness

Loneliness is a dark,
Misery-spreading predator,
Watching out for you in despair.
It is hoping for the lack of someone else's appearance.
He lurks in an area nobody knows of,
But somebody's heard of!
Loneliness is plainly upsetting.

Yusuf Dardouri (10)
Lammack Primary School, Blackburn

Fear

Fear is a black dog
Staring at you with a black pair of eyes
Hiding in a bush
And when a crack is heard
It jumps at you with tremendous force
At your heart to make you feel scared.

Fear is also a black shadow
Leaning over you
And when a scary noise happens it causes it.
It pounces on you with its darkened fingers . . .

Daniel Webster (10)
Lammack Primary School, Blackburn

Fear

Fear is a lonely figure,
Like no other,
Passing you by,
So silently,
It comes by,
But to hurt
And nothing more.
Like a dark figure passing by,
Then I see his face . . .

Matthew Ebbs (10)
Lammack Primary School, Blackburn

Loneliness

Loneliness is a poisonous disease,
Which makes your body invisible.
It blocks your voice box,
The only cure is impossible to find,
As each day passes it gets more deadly,
You're trapped in your own body no one can help you,
No one can hear or see you.

Alia Malik
Lammack Primary School, Blackburn

Fear

Fear creeps up on you when you don't expect it to,
It slowly and painfully creeps up your body then,
Without a warning, it takes over you,
Your brain is left unconscious,
Suddenly it takes over you till you have nothing left.
Fear takes you into a world of nothingness,
Suddenly you come back to life,
Fear gives you a pain saying, 'Ha ha, I did this to you.'

Ayaz Patel (10)
Lammack Primary School, Blackburn

Fear

As I walk on my own
With nobody at my side
Fears keep coming to my head
As I walk down the street
People stare
I look blankly back at them
My fears are running wildly
And I don't know what to do
I huddle up in a corner
But what can I do?
It slowly creeps towards me
As I fight my way through.

Humaira Musa (11)
Lammack Primary School, Blackburn

Loneliness

I look back, jealous of the families
All going out together,
As I walk through the park,
Wishing that I had a family,
I walk over to the swing, tears of loneliness in my eyes,
I break into a run, a feeling of hatred in my heart,
I jump onto the swing, hoping I could fall into Heaven
I am all alone, with no one to go to,
Loneliness is a creature sniffing around hopefully,
Sniffing hopefully for a family to take me away

The feeling overpowers me as I swing all alone . . .

Hennah Patel (10)
Lammack Primary School, Blackburn

Jealousy!

There's a feeling spinning through my head.
Is it anger?
My body burning with fire,
Biting me!

'Why did he break my heart?'
Jealousy says.
Before love was the sun shining brightly!

But now the dark clouds
Of jealousy
Override it!

Sadeya Abhujl (11)
Lammack Primary School, Blackburn

Sounds

I heard a blackbird welcoming the dawn
I heard a shooting star falling to Earth
I heard a soft snowflake landing on a path
I heard a flower blossoming in the sun
I heard a baby giggle at his mum
I heard the giant Earth settling down to sleep
I heard an ice cream van stop up the street
I heard the wind blowing strongly round my house
I heard a big crowd screaming at a goal
I heard mums chattering in the playground
I hear the TV on in a large room
I heard swaying trees dropping coloured leaves
I heard voices shouting loudly in the classroom
I heard growling dogs barking at our ball
I heard echoes along the long dirty road
I heard shrieking owls along the rough walk.

Maisie Nicholson (9)
Lees Hill Primary School, Brampton

In The Night

In the night I saw . . .
A tiny sliver of a shiny moon,
Like all the cheese had been eaten.
A little black bat flying through the cold darkness,
A tabby cat, with shining yellow eyes, creeping along a
Creaking branch.

In the night I heard . . .
An owl in the darkness, hooting away,
A horse galloping up the sloping field towards the gate
To be fed,
The mooing of cows, and the bleating of lambs calling
For their mothers.

In the morning I saw . . .
A flock of birds flying to a telephone wire,
A gaggle of geese flying south for the winter,
A school of fish when I was down by the river.

In the morning I heard . . .
Newly born yellow fluffy chicks cheeping for their mother,
Birds pushing each other out of the nest to be the first
To get food
Ducks calling for their ducklings to get out of the water.

Alice Hudson (10)
Lees Hill Primary School, Brampton

The Best Sister In The World

My sister is a dream when she cares and loves me.
My sister is a rat sometimes but that is very rare.
My sister has a blanket she nibbles the corner of it.
My sister drinks a lot of Coke and always begs for more.
My sister has a special chair and if anyone sits on it
She will growl at them!
My sister is very cross when she's late for gym.
This is my sister!

Rachel Riddle (8)
Lees Hill Primary School, Brampton

Woodpecker

As it lay there, still and silent,
I wondered about its life.
It was young, it had dull feathers.
Was it on its first flight?
How did it feel in that soaring moment of triumph?
What was on the other side of the window that ended its life?

As it lay there, dumb and deaf,
I wondered about its life.
Its feet were curled, it had bent them in flight.
Did it realise its mistake?
Was it trying to turn away?
How did it hit the ground?

As it lay there, stiff and straight,
I wondered about its life.
What a waste of life, what opportunity missed.
Did it ever drill into a golden tree?
Had it dreamed of having a mate?
Did it want to be a parent?

As it lay there, flat and fallen,
I wondered about its life.
It was decaying, melting away.
What would happen to it now?
When it was buried,
How long would it stay
Before disappearing completely?

Isobel Mortimer (10)
Lees Hill Primary School, Brampton

I Love The Taste Of . . .

I love the taste of . . .
Burger smothered in cheese.
Of sweet strawberries covered in whipped cream.
The taste of chocolate cake covered in slippery chocolate.

I hate the taste of
Slippery spaghetti
Spam sizzling in the pan.
Mushy peas with gravy.

I love the sight of
John Dear working on the farm.
Birds swooping through the air.
The sight of dogs playing in the garden.

Arran Forster
Lees Hill Primary School, Brampton

The Magic Box

(Based on 'Magic Box' by Kit Wright)

I will put in the box . . .

Two rustles of a dog rolling in its flying basket,
A chop of a fish splashing the water,
And a clash of a magic sword in battle.

I will put in the box . . .

One sniff of a baby's laughter,
A whiff of an old lady's slipper,
And the fragrance of a new rose.

I will put in the box . . .

Three licks of a cold rose thorn,
A bit of an elderly aunt's last word,
And a bite of a golden sun that lights up the corners that hold . . .

Four wings of a dazzling firefly that dances in the black box,
And has tiny real stars that twinkle against its background,
And its hinges are made of pure gold from Lake Lucerne.

Benjamin Armitage (9)
Lightcliffe Preparatory School

The Magic Box

(Based on 'Magic Box' by Kit Wright)

I will put in the box . . .

Nine wishes written in Zulu,
A tasty tip of a glass galaxy and glass gravy,
And some laughter from a hyena.

I will put in the box . . .

The roar of a snake,
And the hiss of a lion,
And two flickers from a black star.

I will put in the box . . .
A delicious line of music,
And a handful of lion's breath,
And the taste of a Zephyr flying by.

My box is gold and silver and has a galaxy of red and blue stars,
On its side is a mysterious lock,
If you dare to look in my box you will find two gold hinges,
And a ball of floating secrets.

Thomas Lathom-Sharp (9)
Lightcliffe Preparatory School

The Magic Box

(Based on 'Magic Box' by Kit Wright)

My box is made of the finest oak wood in Scotland.
The floor is made from pixie dust,
The hinge is made from the Loch Ness monster's jaw.

I will put in my box . . .

A sniff of an electrified dog
The taste of Elvis Presley's music
Some sound of a pure golden eagle's feather.

The smell of a dinosaur's roar
The taste of a choir at Christmas
A sound of screeches from nails down a blackboard.

Thomas Richardson (9)
Lightcliffe Preparatory School

The Magic Box

(Based on 'Magic Box' by Kit Wright)

I will put in my box . . .

A wizard inside an alien spaceship,
The cowboy on a cow,
A witch on a bike.

I will put in my box . . .

A giant lolly coloured in yellow, orange, red and blue,
And the shiniest crystal water palace,
A man dressed as a gorilla.

Red on the bottom with violet straight lines,
The sides are like fire with orange flames,
And it has got multicoloured painting on the lid.

Liam Stedman (9)
Lightcliffe Preparatory School

The Magic Box

(Based on 'Magic Box' by Kit Wright)

I will put in my box . . .
A refreshing ripple of a rushing river at midday in the night,
A taste of the dancing waves in the crystal clear blue
And smell of a nugget of gold.

I will put in my box . . .
A little ladybird laughing as loud as a leopard,
The sound of a hissing multicoloured snake slithering
On the pavement,
The feel of bursting berries.

My box will be styled with fluffy clouds and angels sat on top,
At night the stars twinkle on the lid like shimmering angel dust,
My box is lined with rare golden eagle feathers,
It will have a special, invisible lock that only I can see.
As soon as I open my box, all my bad thoughts come bursting out
                                        and then fly away.

Rachael Currie (9)
Lightcliffe Preparatory School

The Magic Box

(Based on 'Magic Box' by Kit Wright)

I will put in my box . . .

The taste of blackcurrant ink spilt on a silver wolf,
The chocolate pearl of the River Thames,
The howling of a hipogriff in the dainty Caribbean.

I will put in my box . . .

The sound of Mary's lovely voice on a dull winter night,
A dog's delicate laughter on a dark dancing evening,
The smell of warm banana sun on a hot summer day.

My box is made out of a plastic, pale blue pencil sharpener,
If boys open my box they will get shot with lipgloss,
When girls open it they will be able to see a wonderful galaxy
of pink, purple and red stars.

Rebecca Firth (10)
Lightcliffe Preparatory School

The Magic Box

(Based on 'Magic Box' by Kit Wright)

I will put in . . .

The soft sound of summer sights on a fantasy night
Musical mumbling on the moving mountain
The smell of peaceful perfume in paradise parlour.

I will put in . . .

The taste of royal roses that dwell in the harvest heaven
The smell of fairy dust flying round for all to see
The sound of a melting patchy music player.

The box is wooden with pink material over it.
There are silver twinkling diamonds on it spelling Ellie.
There are pink fluffy edges and the lid has a lock on it.
It has a password that only answers to my voice.

Ellie Sloane (9)
Lightcliffe Preparatory School

The Magic Box
(Based on 'Magic Box' by Kit Wright)

I will put in the box . . .

A smell of fish swimming,
The taste of horses winning,
A sound of pink dreams flying.

I will put in the box . . .

The sound of soft hair swaying,
A taste of a palace playing,
A sight of a sizzling snake.

The box is made out of multicoloured silk with secrets on
that only I can see.
On the lid glittery pink and purple stars that glow when it's dark.
The hinges are made from toe bones of a frog,
There is a silver padlock with a gold key.

Emma Shooter (9)
Lightcliffe Preparatory School

The Magic Box
(Based on 'Magic Box' by Kit Wright)

I will put in the box . . .

A sip of Cinderella's sparkling seaweed, silver slippers,
And the taste of clicking shoes on a glittery rainbow,
The fairy tickle of twinkling Tinkerbell on the midnight sun.

I will put in the box . . .

Lipstick ice cream, eyeshadow biscuits and glossy jelly,
Snake spaghetti and fish gill pizza
Rat and rabbit ravioli ends the dish.

Outside the box there's multicoloured falling stars,
With a glowing, pink pearl padlock
And hula dancers in each bright corner with magic dust,
Right at the back my favourite, a gigantic stage with mermaids
dancing on it.

Olivia Wright (9)
Lightcliffe Preparatory School

The Magic Box

(Based on 'Magic Box' by Kit Wright)

I will put in my box . . .

A sound of a soft swan swimming in the singing sea.
A trop of terrible turtles treading on terrified tarantulas.
A bunch of bellowing bears bathing brilliantly.

I will put in my box . . .

The feel of a frightened furry fox stranded on an island
The feel of a slippery silky slimy snake surrounded by
                                                    Shetland ponies.

I will put in my box . . .

The smell of the finest 50 foot flavoured Christmas cake
And the smell of a stinky swamp covered in seaweed.

My magical mysterious box is made from the bluest water
In the universe with five pure buttons on the lid.
The first button turns every colour you could ever think of
The second one has a galaxy of patterns made with blue, red,
                                                    pink and gold.
The third puts on a shield of silver sharp diamonds,
The fourth every type of materials in the world
The fifth opens the spectacular lid.

Beth Burnhill (9)
Lightcliffe Preparatory School

The Phantoms

'Is there anybody in?'
Shouted the fearful traveller.
'I have the diamonds.'
And then he heard the phantom
And then he saw the phantom walk past
As he tripped into the moonlight,
He tripped again and beastly phantom came.
He rode, shouted, 'Help! Help!'
As the phantom chased him.

Cameron Wroot (9)
Lightcliffe Preparatory School

The Magic Box
(Based on 'Magic Box' by Kit Wright)

I will put in my box . . .

The feel of Captain Hook's hook,
A taste of leaping lambs' laughter on a lovely summer's day,
The roaring of a resting rhino in the rain.

I will put in my box . . .

The trumpeting of an elephant eating,
The feeling of a rushing river running away,
One snip of the world's longest hair on the longest day.

I will put in my box . . .

A drop of the Atlantic Ocean,
The sound of a dream calling,
The taste of a python's hiss.

My box is gold and silver with fairy dust sparkles,
Ancient Egyptian markings that nobody can read,
Sparkling water shimmers when it is opened,
My lock is made out of a clear cloud as soft as soft can be,
Spots of the sky and real stars glisten at the side of the box in
the dark night sky.

Lucy Sheard (10)
Lightcliffe Preparatory School

I'm Here

'I'm here! I'm here!' cried the peasant boy.
'I've got it, don't worry,' he said sadly, almost crying
In front of the glum brown door of the misty mansion.
'I'll go and get a doctor,' as he jumped on his horse
And rode away over the hills,
And as he galloped
He heard the cry of wolves in the distance
And he saw the last glimpse of the mansion
Between the shadow of the big oak trees.

Abbygail Robertshaw (9)
Lightcliffe Preparatory School

The Magic Box

(Based on 'Magic Box' by Kit Wright)

I will put in my box . . .

A cake that hums,
Some fireballs from the legendary dragon,
My pot of transparent gold paint.

I will put in my box . . .

The emerald palace,
The sound of dark lightning,
And dust from the flying carpet.

My box is made of dragon skin,
All locks are opaque but this lock is invisible,
It is colourful and shiny.

Hean Yeung-Lee (9)
Lightcliffe Preparatory School

The Magic Box

(Based on 'Magic Box' by Kit Wright)

I will put in the box . . .

The taste of the dancing butterflies,
The dancing and loving flowers in the breeze,
The singing of the waters on the shore.

I will put in the box . . .

The butterflies flutter in the sky,
The singing in the breeze of a weeping willow tree,
A racing horse cluttering on the ground.

My box is made of golden metal with pink, red and yellow patterns
of butterflies.
It has a steaming handle that burns the hands of all who touch it,
except me.

Emma Leonard (10)
Lightcliffe Preparatory School

The Magic Box
(Based on 'Magic Box' by Kit Wright)

I will put in my box . . .

The twinkle of a fairy's wand glistening in the moonlight,
The taste of a pink crystal,
And the shimmer of a green emerald.

I will put in my box . . .

A sound of a dog miaowing and a cat woofing,
A huge hug from a grizzly bear,
And a diamond from the Wizard of Oz.

My box is made of swan's feathers,
Dyed pink, purple and gold,
With bells, hearts and glitter on the lid,
When you open the box lurking in the corners is unicorns' magic,
It has a special lock made of fairy dust that can only be opened by a
magical code.

Danielle North (9)
Lightcliffe Preparatory School

Let Me In!

'Who lives in this old mansion?' screamed the traveller.
'I will pay for my safety from death.'
Banging on the mansion door.
'Why don't you answer me?'
And all he could hear were leaves rustling
And owls hooting.
He saw the owls flying, but no movement in the mansion.
And he saw the man coming closer
To him with the knife out.
Just then the traveller could not see or hear anything . . .

Oliver Firth (10)
Lightcliffe Preparatory School

Autumn Gardens

Crinkly leaves
Falling from the trees
Like confetti.

Small robins
Chirping
Like sweet music.

Sly fox
Creeping around
Like a thief in the night.

Speedy squirrels
Collecting nuts
Like gathering firewood.

Ross MacLeod (9)
Linlithgow Bridge Primary School, Linlithgow

Autumn Gardens

Crinkly leaves,
Falling from the trees
Like confetti in the wind

Tiny field mice
Snug in the wood pile
Like little puppies

Sly foxes
Creeping silently
Like thieves in the night

Shiny conkers
Lying on the ground
Like a pile of pebbles.

Jensen Gardner (9)
Linlithgow Bridge Primary School, Linlithgow

Autumn Gardens

Crinkly leaves
Falling from the trees
Like confetti in the wind.

Sly fox
Creeping about at night
Like a thief in the dark.

Tiny field mice
Snug in a wood pile
Like little cosy puppies.

Bonfires
Sending up sparks
Like shining gold snowflakes.

Cracking conkers
Hanging on trees
Like colourful leaves.

Bright red roses
Ripening in the sun
Like little red dots.

Scurrying squirrels
Running up trees
Like men in a race.

Ben Milne (9)
Linlithgow Bridge Primary School, Linlithgow

Autumn Gardens

Crinkly leaves
Falling from the trees
Like confetti in the wind.

Anxious squirrels
Burying nuts
Like a treasure chest.

Slow snails
Leaving icy trails behind
Like white snow.

Fast mice
Running through hedges
As fast as race cars.

Shooting bonfire sparks
Erupting through the air
Sparkling like stars.

Spiky hedgehogs
Shuffling through the leaves
As quiet as mice.

Madeleine Nicholls (9)
Linlithgow Bridge Primary School, Linlithgow

Autumn Gardens

Crinkly leaves
Falling from the trees
Like rolled up paper.

Anxious squirrels
Burying nuts
Like a treasure chest.

Shiny plants
Sparkling in the moon's shadow
Like diamonds.

Squirming woodlice
Trying to get out of the rain and snow
Like little caterpillars.

Fast mice
Running through the parks
Like the fastest man running.

Slow snails
Squirming their slowest
Trailing slime behind them.

Tiny hedgehogs
Spiking up
Like a big ball of spikes.

Eilidh Stewart (9)
Linlithgow Bridge Primary School, Linlithgow

Autumn Gardens

Juicy red berries
As red as
Blood.

Blooming flowers
As bright as
Light.

Icy waters
Trickling like
Diamonds shimmering in the moonlight.

Crinkly leaves
Falling from the trees like
Confetti in the wind.

Pouncing foxes
Hunting their prey as
Quiet as mice in a church.

Snuffling hedgehogs
Shuffling amongst the leaves like
Animals looking for food.

Squirming squirrels
Eating nuts and conkers like
A woodpecker pecking at a tree.

Hannah McMonagle Johnston (8)
Linlithgow Bridge Primary School, Linlithgow

Autumn Gardens

Crinkly leaves
Falling from the trees
Like confetti in the wind.

Little robins tweeting
Tweeting so quietly
Like piano music.

Black berries
Ripening hour by hour
Like shining jewels.

Sly fox
Sneaking around
Like a dark witch.

Fireworks
Sparking up into the air
Like stars in the great, night sky.

Hannah Johnston (9)
Linlithgow Bridge Primary School, Linlithgow

Autumn Gardens

Crinkly leaves
Falling from the trees
Like confetti in the wind

Red robins
Tweeting in their nest
Like sweet music

Sweet berries
Hanging on the bush
Like bright red roses

Juicy brambles
Hanging on the branches
Like shiny red rubies.

Catherine Wilson (9)
Linlithgow Bridge Primary School, Linlithgow

Autumn Gardens

Crinkly leaves
Falling from the trees
Like confetti in the wind.

Tiny bats
Flying in the midnight sky
Like dots.

Slimy slugs
Slithering around
As squishy as jelly.

Cracking conkers
Falling from trees
As fast as shooting stars.

Bare trees
Twisting and turning
Like water slides.

Catriona Charlton (9)
Linlithgow Bridge Primary School, Linlithgow

Autumn Gardens

Crinkly leaves
Falling from the trees
Like confetti in the wind

Red robins
Tweeting in their nest
Like sweet music

Sweet berries
Hanging on a bush
Like bright red jewels

Shiny conkers
Lying on the ground
Like dark brown cricket balls.

Catherine Tuckett (9)
Linlithgow Bridge Primary School, Linlithgow

Autumn Gardens

Crinkly leaves
Falling from trees
Like confetti in the wind.

Slimy snails
Moving slowly
Like tortoises.

Little rabbits
Running fast
Like boys in a race.

Tiny robins
Chirping loudly
Like piano music.

Shiny conkers
Lying around
Like brand new shoes.

Crispy leaves
On the ground
Like scrunched up paper.

Brambles and berries
Glowing bright
As stars at night.

Spiky hedgehogs
Hurrying fast
Like cars on the motorway.

Small caterpillars
Wriggling in the earth
Like tiny beetles.

Little black bats
Swooping through the air
Like little black dots.

Brambles and berries
Swaying in bushes
As red as blood.

Funny frogs
Hopping about
Like girls on a pogo-stick

Small centipedes
Scuttling and small
Like moving eggs.

Tiny snails
Slimy and brown
As slugs.

Kate Harrower (9)
Linlithgow Bridge Primary School, Linlithgow

Autumn Gardens

Crinkly leaves
Falling from the trees
Like confetti in the wind.

Little robins
Tweeting loudly
Like our school choir.

Rosy red berries
Dangling very high up
Like Mum's new roses.

Shiny conkers
Lying low on the ground
Like brand new shoes.

Sly foxes
Creeping around
Like dark, black robbers.

Cold breezes
Blowing everywhere
Like a winter visitor.

Dark bats
Sitting on rooftops
Like suspicious black dots.

Alison Tulloch (9)
Linlithgow Bridge Primary School, Linlithgow

Autumn Gardens

Crinkly leaves
Falling from the trees
Like little brown snowflakes

Slimy slugs
Slithering along the ground
Like a snowboarder

Shiny conkers
Bursting open every minute of the day
Like a tiny little baby

Juicy brambles
Falling off the trees
Squirting red juice

Spiky hedgehogs
Guilty in the ground
Like spikes on a brush

Croaking frogs
Jumping from stone to stone
Like little gymnasts

Sly foxes
Guilty as can be
Like thieves in the night.

Gemma Samson (9)
Linlithgow Bridge Primary School, Linlithgow

Autumn Gardens

Crinkly leaves
Falling from the trees
Like confetti in the wind.

Sly fox
Creeping about at night
Like a thief in the dark.

Tiny field mice
Snug in a wooden pile
Like little cosy puppies.

Bonfires
Sending up sparks
Like shiny gold snowflakes.

Cracking conkers
Hanging onto trees
Like coloured leaves.

Bright red roses
Ripening in the sun
Like little dots of ink.

Scurrying squirrels
Running up trees
Like men in a race.

Andrew MacDonald (9)
Linlithgow Bridge Primary School, Linlithgow

Autumn Gardens

Crinkly leaves
As crinkly as crisp
Packets in the wind.

Fluffy squirrels
Sleeping in the trees
As fluffy as soft wool.

Spiky hedgehogs
Rolling across the grass
As prickly as needles.

Singing birds
Singing like angels
In the sky.

Shiny conkers
Falling off trees
As hard as bricks.

Michael Currie (9)
Linlithgow Bridge Primary School, Linlithgow

Autumn

Crinkly leaves
Falling from the trees
Like confetti in the wind

Crispy leaves
Lying on the ground
Like scrunched up paper

Slimy slugs
Moving about
Like slithering snakes

Juicy brambles
Hanging on bushes
Like a red tomato

Rosy red berries
Hanging on the bushes
Like splodges of paint.

Ardal Miller (9)
Linlithgow Bridge Primary School, Linlithgow

Autumn Gardens

Crunchy leaves
Lying on the ground
As crunchy as biscuits.

Brambles and berries
Hanging on a bush
With juice as red as blood.

Plump toads
Hiding under logs
As round as balloons.

Spiky hedgehogs
Hibernating quietly
With their branches spiky as nails.

Slimy slugs
Slowly leaving
Shimmering like diamonds.

Sly foxes
Out at night
Creeping as quietly as mice.

Strong conkers
Falling off trees
As hard as bricks.

Slow snails
Sauntering along the path
As slow as babies.

Damp logs
Lying on the lawn
As still as statues.

Biting midges
Drinking blood
Sucking like evil vampires.

Pitch-black bats
In the air
Flapping like birds.

Tall trees
Swaying in the wind
As gracefully as a ballerina.

Flying birds
Eating bread
Like pigs.

Tiny field mice
Snug in a wood pile
Like piglets in a sty.

Joanna Boxall (9)
Linlithgow Bridge Primary School, Linlithgow

Autumn Scene

Crinkly leaves
Falling from the trees
Like confetti in the wind

Spiky hedgehogs
Sitting in the garden
As jagged as needles

Soggy grass
Sitting wet
As a massive puddle

Shiny conkers
Falling off trees
As fast as wind

Slimy snails
Leaving slime tracks
Like juice spread along the ground

Colourful trees
With lots of leaves
Shaking like jelly

Dead flowers
Hanging over the mud
Like tiny leaves on a tree hanging over.

Daniel Beaton (9)
Linlithgow Bridge Primary School, Linlithgow

Autumn Gardens

Crinkly leaves
Falling from the trees
Like confetti in the wind

Spiky hedgehogs
Sitting in the garden
As jagged as needles

Shiny conkers
Falling off trees
As fast as wind

Soggy grass
Sitting wet
Like a massive puddle

Slimy slugs
Leaving slimy tracks
Like juice spread on the ground

Colourful trees
With lots of leaves
Shaking like banana shake

Dead flowers
Hanging over the mud
Like a tree that's fallen to the ground.

Ross Cruickshanks (9)
Linlithgow Bridge Primary School, Linlithgow

Autumn Gardens

Crinkly leaves
Falling from trees
Like confetti in the wind.

Cracking conkers
Falling from trees
Falling from trees as strong as bricks.

Burrowing badgers
Getting ready to hibernate
Digging as fast as diggers.

Scattered berries
Falling like asteroids
Splodged on the ground like paint.

Slimy rocks
At the bottom of the garden
Rotting like old bananas.

Red-breasted robins
Flying high
Tweeting like wonderful music.

Juicy berries
Squirting juice as they fall
Squirting juice like a fizzed up can.

Harriet Reeder (9)
Linlithgow Bridge Primary School, Linlithgow

Autumn Gardens

Crinkly leaves
Falling from the trees
Like confetti in the wind.

Tiny bats
Fly in the midnight sky
Like dots.

Slimy slugs
Slithering around
As squishy as jelly.

Cracking conkers
Falling from trees
As fast as shooting stars.

Bare trees
Twisting and turning
Like water slides.

Barbara Hogan (9)
Linlithgow Bridge Primary School, Linlithgow

Autumn Garden

Crinkly leaves
Falling from the trees
Like confetti in the wind.

Fluffy squirrels
Sleeping in trees
As fluffy as wool.

Spiky hedgehogs
Rolling across the ground
As prickly as needles.

Singing birds
Flying high
Like jet planes.

Shiny conkers
Falling from trees
As hard as bricks.

Cameron Atkinson (9)
Linlithgow Bridge Primary School, Linlithgow

Autumn Gardens

Crinkly leaves
Falling from the trees
Like confetti in the wind.

Chirping robins
Chirping loudly
Like car alarms.

Spiky hedgehogs
Curled up tightly
As spiky as knives.

Sly foxes
Sneaking around
Like thieves in the night.

Juicy berries
Growing on the tree
Shining blood-red.

Slow snails
Sliding along
Like slithering snakes on ice.

Spotty ladybirds
Flying about
Like toadstools in the sky.

Alice Newey (9)
Linlithgow Bridge Primary School, Linlithgow

Autumn Gardens

Crinkly leaves
Falling from the trees
Like confetti in the wind

Pitch-black bats
Flying off the roofs
As black as night.

Slimy slugs
Leaving trails
Like sticky glue.

Juicy brambles
Hanging on bushes
Like red tomatoes.

Sly foxes
Sneaking about
Like burglars.

Daniel Nimmo (9)
Linlithgow Bridge Primary School, Linlithgow

Crocodile

Crocodiles are sly and patient
The crocodile creeps through the river slowly,
Waiting for his meal
The crocodile sees something!
Zebra is scared
Snatch!
He's gone!

Elizabeth Richards (8)
Lyndon Preparatory School, Colwyn Bay

Colour Poem

What is pink?
My room is pink with my curtains.
What is blue?
The door is blue with numbers on it.
What is red?
The carpet is red with patterns.
What is green?
The hairspray's green with writing on it.
What is yellow?
The Simpsons are yellow with big eyes.
What is purple?
My shirt is purple with sparkly words.
What is ginger?
My cat is ginger with furry stripes.
What is multcoloured?
The rainbow is multicoloured in the sky on a rainy day.

Lorna Dunn (10)
Melbourne Park Primary School, Chelmsford

My Playground Poem

P layground people play
L augh loudly and lively
A rguing and active
Y elling year after year
G rowing gorgeous plants
R osy cheeks when we come into the classroom
O utside objects move
U nhurt children play
N ever boring
D elighted playground poem.

Erin Parkhurst (8)
Melbourne Park Primary School, Chelmsford

My Senses Poem

I like to feel my snow-white teddy bear
When I'm feeling down.

I like to hear the sound of my MP3 player
When I get home from school.

I like to see snow on a cold winter's day
To play in.

I like to smell my dad's cooking on a weekend night
When I am starving.

I like the taste of Indian food
When it's dished up on really big plates.

I like the sound of the wind
As I whizz on my bike.

I like the taste of curries
When my dad makes them hot and spicy.

Abigail Loble (10)
Melbourne Park Primary School, Chelmsford

Playground Poem

P eople play games
L oud people scream
A nd children argue with each other
Y elling people give you a headache
G ood people help the teacher
R acket all around
O ver the playground there are trees
U nbelievable things happen to the children
N asty people bully good ones
D ancing girls show off to the boys.

Keeleigh Hammond (8)
Melbourne Park Primary School, Chelmsford

My Senses Poem On Lasagne

I like the feel of hot lasagne on my plate
Waiting for me to put it in my tummy.

I like the sound of rock and roll
To imagine my lasagne dancing.

I like to see hot tasty lasagne
Steaming up my nose.

I like to smell lasagne being cooked
By my Super Lasagne Mummy.

I like the taste of lasagne
With its hot and creamy flavour.

My favourite dinner on the big plate
Is a cheesy flavour lasagne.

That's why my mum goes to Iceland every day!

Jamie Ripton (10)
Melbourne Park Primary School, Chelmsford

Playgrounds

Playgrounds are a perfect place to hide-and-seek
People playing football and scoring goals
'Please play with me, Josh.'
'Yes I will play with you.'
I wish I could play all day
'Do you want to play with me?'
'Yes I do.'
'Let's play 'it'.'
Painting bright collages in chalk together
Losing track of my friends
Playing hopscotch together makes it fun
Can you wait to play all day?

Alexander Sullivan (9)
Melbourne Park Primary School, Chelmsford

Senses Poem

I like to feel a sharp tip of a pen while I'm writing.

I like to hear the sound of a computer whirling
While it's loading.

I like to see birthday cakes with lit candles
As they flicker in the dark.

I like to smell fresh cut grass in our garden
When it has just been cut.

I like the taste of lemon as I suck sherbet out.

I like to listen to MTV music on Sky TV
With my friends.

I like to eat cold chocolate chip ice cream after dinner.

Bradley Mardell (10)
Melbourne Park Primary School, Chelmsford

Colour Poem

What is red?
My lunch box is red filled with my favourite food.
What is blue?
My dad's car when he whizzes down the road.
What is black?
My socks are black in my black shoes.
What is white?
My piece of paper is white when I haven't written on it.
What is brown?
My grandad's dog called Tam
She is brown when she has rolled in the mud.
What is green?
My house is green when it's painted in the spring.

Billy Buckingham (11)
Melbourne Park Primary School, Chelmsford

Snooker Senses Poem

I like to feel the snooker cue slipping through my fingers.
I like to hear the sound of the click of the balls
As they hit each other.
I like to see the ball go straight through the snooker hole.
I like the smell of the chalk as I twist the tip of the cue.
I like the taste of the success when I win a game.
I like the feel of the trophy as I hold it high over my head,
When I win the championship.

Anthony Reval (10)
Melbourne Park Primary School, Chelmsford

The Playground

Playgrounds are the perfect place to be
Children playing football, basketball and hockey
Speeding past like Grand Prix racers
Jumping on the hopscotch like a leaping frog
Come on let's join in
But all too soon it's time to go in.

Josh Cormack-Butler (9)
Melbourne Park Primary School, Chelmsford

Playground

P lay on the equipment
L aughter in the houses
A shley and Daniel climb the wall
Y ou and me having fun in the school fair
G irls always giggling
R unning on the field
O ther people come and play
U nder the breezy trees
N obody falls out
D o as you are told.

Ashley Gorham (7)
Melbourne Park Primary School, Chelmsford

Playground Poem

I hear children screaming 'Goal!'
As the ball crosses the line.
I hear children talking about a sleepover.
I see people playing happily.
I see people playing excitedly as the play equipment comes out.
Friends help me when I'm hurt.
I feel happy as the people play happily together.

Kaylem Skitch (9)
Melbourne Park Primary School, Chelmsford

Playground Poem

In the playground
I hear children playing excitedly with their friends
I hear screaming loudly
I hear children quickly jumping on the playground
Children are playing in the playground
I feel happy
Friends are kind, sad, jealous, laughing, and telling jokes.

Lachlan Stanley (7)
Melbourne Park Primary School, Chelmsford

In The Playground

P ull myself on the pole
L ike a clever brown monkey
A nd spin around the big pole all day long
Y ou all listen and learn
G o around having fun nicely and carefully
R un, jump, learn and play
O thers distribute cards at Christmas in the playground
U mpire the games we play at break time
N o one will be silly in class
D elight everyone you know students.

Daniel Potter
Melbourne Park Primary School, Chelmsford

In the Playground

P eople making new friends, karate kicking, new playing
L aughter spreading, fun playing with new people
A mazing, new friends playing with me
Y ellow sun shining in my eyes
G iggling girls joking around queuing up for the climbing frame
R unning around speeding like a motorbike
O bjects to be found
U nder the tree, me and my friends
N oises to be heard
D isco dancing with my friends
S kipping with my friends.

Kaycee O'Sullivan (8)
Melbourne Park Primary School, Chelmsford

Friends

In the playground, I hear children happily singing in the rain.
I feel cold because the wind is blowing.
Friends are skipping quietly together.
I see flowers blowing in the wind slowly.

Katy Edwards (7)
Melbourne Park Primary School, Chelmsford

In The Playground

P layground, you can play in it
L et's see who can bounce their ball the highest
A nd now let's run like the wind
Y elling friends, yelling help
G reat friends are helpful
R un away
O xygen is good for the lungs
U ses the best play equipment
N ow let's go
D o you have fun?

Kurtis Mclaren (8)
Melbourne Park Primary School, Chelmsford

In The Playground

I feel loved by my girlfriend
I feel cheerful to be in the playground.

I hear children singing softly to their friends.
I hear children chatting to best friends.

I see children sprinting across the playground
I see happy children laughing with their mates.

Friends are helpful friends that care for you.

Charley Gorham (9)
Melbourne Park Primary School, Chelmsford

Playgrounds

Playgrounds you are so big
I could play all day
I cannot wait to play
Who is that? It is my friend
Crawl on the floor
Jump in the sky
Run like the wind.

Jack Muir (9)
Melbourne Park Primary School, Chelmsford

In The Playground

P lay with my friends
L aughing makes us happy
A llowed to play ball
Y ou can play with me
G oing out to play, it is fun
R unning keeps us fit
O ur feet keep us on the ground
U nder the trees keeps us cool
N eeding your friends
D aniel and Ashley playing ball.

Daniel Ripton (8)
Melbourne Park Primary School, Chelmsford

In The Playground

P laying all day long
L etting others play
A nd they let me as well
Y ou can play
G round is what is wet
R ules on the equipment
O utside when it is wet
U sing the trees for shade
N ew people join our school
D ogs barking at the gate.

Melissa Eden (8)
Melbourne Park Primary School, Chelmsford

Senses Poem

I like to feel my cat at night when I am going to sleep.
I like to see my mum when I hurry home from school.
I like to hear my birds sing in the afternoon.
I like to smell my mum's cooking while I am watching television.
I like to taste my dad's cooking and he likes to taste mine.

Mercedes Babij (10)
Melbourne Park Primary School, Chelmsford

In The Playground

P laying with my skipping rope with my friends
L aughing so much we can't help rolling about on the field
A nd then we go indoors to do some writing
Y ou can't help biting your nails thinking how funny playtime was
G reat now it's time to settle down and do some work
R eady for action is the way to be when it's time to do PE
O ver and over the equipment we go
U nderneath all the hard work I'm still thinking of the playground
N o more laughing, I must get on with working
D o spend time on the playground; it's a fun place to be.

Kelli-Ann Chapman (7)
Melbourne Park Primary School, Chelmsford

The Playground

P lay with me please
L ight-hearted always
A llowed out
Y oung children playing 'It'
G lum sometimes
R un yourself, you are in
O ut and about
U ndercover games
N ever unhappy
D ash about.

James Carter (8)
Melbourne Park Primary School, Chelmsford

Colour Poem

Red is like a fireball flying through the sky.
Blue is like a tidal wave in the sea.
Green is like a land of fresh green grass.
Orange is like an orange without its skin.
Yellow is like the sun on a hot day.

Ryan Moore (9)
Melbourne Park Primary School, Chelmsford

The Playground

Playing in the snow
Lay in the trees
About playing with a new person
You like to play with me?
Go inside with someone
Running around like 'Looney Tunes'
On and on with people
No one wants to play with me
Do you want to play with me?

Yes I do.

Liam Brown (9)
Melbourne Park Primary School, Chelmsford

My Playground Poem

I hear children playing with their friends calmly
Friends are giggly chatting with their mates
I see children giving friendship tokens
I feel the wind blowing on my hands on a summer's day.

Tommy Silvey (8)
Melbourne Park Primary School, Chelmsford

In The Playground

P eople playing football on the playground
L oud shouting with children playing games
A nd fast running races to the bench
Y es we can all play together
G reat fun with the skipping ropes
R acing around the field as fast as we can
O utside getting fresh air
U nder the oak tree to find some shade
N ow time to go back in class
D inner time is over, get back to our work.

Jessica Little (7)
Melbourne Park Primary School, Chelmsford

In The Playground

In the playground I hear children running around
Very happy with their friends.
I see children crying because they have no one to play with.
I feel very happy because my friends want to play with me.
Friends are there for you when you're blue.

Lauren-Ann Hart (8)
Melbourne Park Primary School, Chelmsford

My Senses Poem

I like to feel the snow crunching in my hand on a cold winter's day.

I like the sound of children saying 'You can't get me!'
In a snowball fight.

I like to see others smiling on Christmas Day while opening
His or her presents.

I like the smell of roast turkey cooking in the oven
For the Christmas feast.

I like the taste of hot chocolate on Christmas Day.

I like the feel of the snowflakes landing and then
Melting on my hand.

ᐧI like to see a great Christmas poem by me.

Levi-Wayne Stanley (9)
Melbourne Park Primary School, Chelmsford

Renga Poems About Christmas

Christmas is coming
It may be a white Christmas
Christmas is the best.

Christmas is so nice
Christmas time is the best day
Giving is so good.

Christmas is so great
Christmas is so wonderful
Christmas time is fun.

I like to get cards
I like to open presents
I like Christmas time.

Andrew Pearce (10)
Melbourne Park Primary School, Chelmsford

Senses Poem

I like to feel my dog because it is fluffy and scruffy and warm.
I like to see my rabbits after school every day.
I like to hear my mum's car when it is on.
I like to smell my roast dinner on a Sunday night.
I like to taste melted chocolate in my mouth.

Jennifer Clark (10)
Melbourne Park Primary School, Chelmsford

Senses Poem

I like to feel my beanbag
When I am gazing at my television.

I like to see my cat snuggling
Up to my other cats.

I like to hear my cats purring
When they are cheerful.

I like to smell the green grass
When it is enjoyable and fresh.

I like to taste Minstrels as they melt in my mouth
And the crack that lets the chocolate burst out.

Steven Drew (10)
Melbourne Park Primary School, Chelmsford

Friends

In the playground
I hear children shouting out loudly to Amy.
I see children skipping happily
Friends are playing happily near the tree
I feel good because everyone's playing excitedly.

Emma Hope (8)
Melbourne Park Primary School, Chelmsford

Playground Poem

In the playground
I hear children playing quietly
I hear children playing loudly.

In the playground
I see people playing football nicely
I see people playing kindly.

In the playground
Friends are kind to me when I am hurt
Friends are kind when they let me play with them.

In the playground
I feel happy when I make a new friend
I feel happy when my friends play with me.

Ashman Elles (8)
Melbourne Park Primary School, Chelmsford

Playground Poem

In the playground
I can hear children
Playing with the teacher.

In the playground
I can hear children
Running happily
To the wall.

In the playground
Friends are giving friendship tokens.

In the playground I can see
Children playing happily.

In the playground
I feel loved by my boyfriend!

Kiera Cagney (8)
Melbourne Park Primary School, Chelmsford

A Renja Poem About Christmas

Winter is so cold
I play in the snow a lot.
Christmas here again.

I love Christmas time.
Christmas is in December.
I get lots of cards.

Christmas is the best
Because you can make snowmen.
The streets are all white.

My friends like Christmas
My Christmas tree's very tall.
My mum cooks dinner.

I like my tree lights.
People think Christmas is dumb.
Christmas lights are bright.

It is lots of fun
Opening presents is cool
I like Christmas lights.

Giving is friendly
My friends appreciate gifts
I get lovely gifts.

I love Christmas Day
Can't wait for Christmas dinner,
Or for my pudding.

Laura Theedom (9)
Melbourne Park Primary School, Chelmsford

In The Playground

In the playground I hear children giggling happily with their friends.
In the playground I see children sprinting.
I feel happy because I have friends to play with.
In the playground friends are good and they are kind.

Tanya Jervis (7)
Melbourne Park Primary School, Chelmsford

In The Playground

I see children doing skipping happily.
Friends give you friendship tokens.
I see children sprinting happily across the playground.
I hear children excitedly talking.
I feel giggly when someone makes a joke.
Friends are for cheering you up when you are down.

Courtney Clarke (8)
Melbourne Park Primary School, Chelmsford

In The playground

In the playground
I feel joyful in the playground.

In the playground
I see people racing with their friends.

In the playground
I hear children giggling

In the playground.
Friends are kind to friends.

Nigel Stratford (9)
Melbourne Park Primary School, Chelmsford

My Playground Poem

In the playground
I hear children singing beautifully round the tree.
Friends are caring for me.
I see children skipping fast and slow, joyfully with their friends.
I feel so excited when I'm caring.
I hear children chatting about a sleepover.

Shannon Grinstead (8)
Melbourne Park Primary School, Chelmsford

Playground Poem

I hear children playing excitedly with their friends.
In the playground I hear children screaming loudly.
I see children playing in the playground happily.
I feel happy.
Friends are laughing happily together.

Ashley Byford (8)
Melbourne Park Primary School, Chelmsford

Untitled

I see someone climbing on the bars, someone sprinting.
I hear children singing softly by the tree.
Friends are funny.
I feel good because my friends are in a race
And they are winning.

Daniel Coleman (7)
Melbourne Park Primary School, Chelmsford

In The Playground

I hear children playing in the playground
I see ice on the leaves, friends from other classes,
Teachers talking, friendly
Friends are fun to play with.
I feel sad.

Luke Brown (7)
Melbourne Park Primary School, Chelmsford

The Snow

I can make people cold,
And I can be fun.

I can help you make snowmen
Or get in a fight.

I can look like Heaven
But can't go up to the sun.

I can make people upset
And I can be great snowballs.

Some people don't like me
But I can transform into angels.

Making people happy feels great
But when I make people upset
I feel down.

But overall - I'm just great fun!

Hannah Ford (10)
Oaklands Primary School, Welwyn

Hannah The Hamster

Hannah the hamster has ears like crystals.
Her teeth are the prickles on a green leaved bush.

Her tail is wagging and swaying in the breeze.
Her nose is a black, old, rotten ball.

She likes sleeping on hay.
When she runs about she's like a wild beast.

When she sleeps she squeaks all night
Then she wakes with a rustling noise.

Philippa Stephens (7)
Oaklands Primary School, Welwyn

Fire

I can burn myself and take ages and ages,
I can spread my heat for miles and miles.

I can steal in and not wake the alarm,
I can run free along the ground.

Accidents I can cause without any harm,
Or ring the siren to maximum alarm.

Then rage, like the waves going backwards or forwards,
And carry on until I'm small and finally under control.

Smoke I can bring all wrapped in a parcel,
Then make you cough and choke for hours and hours.

Finally a trip to A and E for weeks and weeks,
Maybe forever.

Katherine Woods (10)
Oaklands Primary School, Welwyn

The Bat

Betty the bat has ears like liquorice.
Her teeth are sharp pencils in a plastic pencil pot.

Her back's blowing like a rug on the washing line.
Her nose is a rubbery ping-pong ball.

Her feet like a leaf on a bush.
She screeches like an eagle in the dark blue sky.

Then she swoops through the sky.
She glides like an aeroplane through the clouds.

She sleeps up on the old dead tree.
Then she wakes with a stretch and a yawn.

Laura Goodacre (7)
Oaklands Primary School, Welwyn

Wonderful Wind

I can make you wrap up warm,
And push you along your way.

I can creep into your house,
Whilst being as timid as a mouse.

I can run upstairs,
So I can see the flowers.

I can scatter seeds,
Or make a noise with reeds.

I can be very quiet,
But I can also rage and riot.

I can sleep all day,
I can sleep all night,
But when I wake up you don't want
To be where I am . . .

Hannah Kempster (9)
Oaklands Primary School, Welwyn

The Cat

Honey the cat has ears like snow.
His back is as fluffy as a ball of wool.

Teeth like needles in a new sewing kit.
His tail you'd call a long candy cane.

He cries like a baby.
His nose is as wet as an old pink ball.

When he's asleep he snores like a pig.
Then he wakes you with a friendly lick.

Zara Hoy (7)
Oaklands Primary School, Welwyn

Katie's Cat

Cara the cat has ears like feathers,
She has shiny sharp teeth like fangs.

Her miaow is a baby crying,
Her tail you'd call a scrunched up rope with a motor inside.

She sleeps on a smooth rock-bed,
And purrs when she wakes up.

Katie Genever (7)
Oaklands Primary School, Welwyn

James The Gerbil

James the gerbil has ears like black beans,
And teeth like the point of a pyramid.

His back is like an old black dustbin,
He has claws like the night.

When he sleeps he is quiet like mice,
Then he wakes and is as bright as the sun.

Robert Drew (7)
Oaklands Primary School, Welwyn

Cara The Cat

Cara the cat has ears like a kitten.
Teeth like knives, a drawer of metal.

His back's black fur on a dark blue sky,
His tail is a rat's tail, beats it like a drum.

He purrs like a kitten in the beautiful sun.
When he sleeps he purrs and dreams.

Then he wakes you with a thump.

Ben Wilson (7)
Oaklands Primary School, Welwyn

I Have An Oasis

I have a land of Lego
It is on my shelf
And I could build
Just like an elf.

> Build as high as the clouds
> Away from my brother
> And all my stress
> Build all and other.

Away from envy
Building more than you could imagine
Making planes and cars
And life on Mars.

> Breaking it down
> And making it taller
> Making extras
> That are even smaller.

Robert White (8)
Oaklands Primary School, Welwyn

Jerry The Tiger

Jerry the tiger has ears like a duvet,
Teeth like the points of twenty pencils.

His eyes are like a squishy toy,
The colour of fur is bright orange and black.

His nose is as wet as the beautiful sea,
His paws are very rough.

His tail is as hard as a brown book,
His leg is as straight as a ruler.

When he sleeps at night he rolls on the floor,
Then he wakes and yawns.

William Vaughan (7)
Oaklands Primary School, Welwyn

Adam The Alligator

Adam the alligator is as fat as a tree,
Teeth like splinters of spiky wood.

His tail you'd run away from,
His nose is a long stick.

His back's a rocky, bumpy stone,
He's like a robot when he walks.

When he sleeps he blows bubbles when he snores.
Then he wakes up with a yawn of breath.

Adam Webster (7)
Oaklands Primary School, Welwyn

Tigger The Tiger

Tigger the tiger has teeth like needles.
His tail is a snake with a motor inside.

His nose is a pink squashy ball.
His back is strips of gold and white card.

He sounds like a squeaky old hinge.
When he sleeps he yawns like our growling heater.

Then he wakes you with a sharp, loud roar.

Katie Deards (7)
Oaklands Primary School, Welwyn

Harry The Hamster

Harry the hamster has ears like pillows,
His nose is the rubber of an old pink ball.

His back's a golden summery sky,
He squeaks like a rusty, old, squeaky bike.

When he sleeps, he's as cosy as a warm bed,
Then he wakes with a wash of tongue.

Alastair Drew (7)
Oaklands Primary School, Welwyn

The Draught

I can travel over a bike but not knock it over
Or run through a living room but not make a noise.

I can see for miles and miles without people noticing
Or make a chill run through your spine because I'm cold.

I can rustle through trees and make them huddle up and run
Through anything without you knowing.

I can stand up properly like all humans do
But when I'm worn out I can no longer blow on storms.

I'm around all day running through the air conditioners
And warm you up as Mum gets rid of the frost.

I can create catastrophes and create disasters
Or end your play at school by making it snow.

I can make a decision like all humans do, I have a heart just like you.

Connor Wilson (9)
Oaklands Primary School, Welwyn

Danny The Dolphin

Danny the dolphin has ears like pots.
Teeth like sharks of the deep blue sea.

His back is like a smooth, papery book,
Soft bed, hard bed, floating by.

His nose is a plastic water bottle, gurgling down,
His tail you'd call a flapping fin with a motor inside.

He clicks like a human laughing away.
When he sleeps he floats around making noises that are found.

When he swims he swims like a jet.
Then he leaps like a tidal wave.

Bethany Kendle (8)
Oaklands Primary School, Welwyn

Georgia The Guinea Pig

Georgia the guinea pig has ears like coins.
Eyes like the stars in the shining sky.

Her back's a brownish autumn leaf.
Her nose is like a tiny pink teddy.

Feet like needles in a sewing box.
When she sleeps she squeaks like a mouse.

Then she wakes and plays on her wheel.

Cara Beard (8)
Oaklands Primary School, Welwyn

Bob The Dog

Bob the dog has ears like mugs,
Teeth like splinters from dented wood spikes.

His back is a sticky white snowflake
With a touch of golden toffee.

He has a spongy wet nose
That moves when he breathes.

He sleeps like a baby,
Then he wakes you with a loud bark.

Jamie Kempster (8)
Oaklands Primary School, Welwyn

Dangerous Animals

Adam the alligator has teeth like shiny needles,
His nose is like two dark tunnels in the night.

He walks like a stiff metal robot,
Tail like spiky pencil tips.

He snores like paint pots squirting out paint,
When he runs it is like a football rolling really fast.

Vishva Naik (8)
Oaklands Primary School, Welwyn

Robby The Rabbit

Robby the rabbit has ears like soft silk,
Teeth as white as snow flint.

His tail is a furry cotton ball of fluff,
His nose is a bright pink marshmallow.

When he sleeps he's as quiet as mice,
When he wakes he shuffles about.

Jessica Hall (7)
Oaklands Primary School, Welwyn

Matt The Rat

Matt the rat has ears like hair,
His teeth are like a sharp blowing wind.

His back's a hairy bear stomping in the wood,
His nose is a pink ping-pong ball.

A shaved-off tiny tail that came off with the sound of a wail,
Dark, red-eyed, he whimpers like twenty wolves.

When he growls it's a scary sound
That bites through mornings and nights.

When he sleeps it's a noisy snore
That wakes you with a spike of his claws.

Daniel Rice (8)
Oaklands Primary School, Welwyn

Gus The Pup

Gus the pup has ears like plugs.
His back is a squashy marshmallow, soft and snowy white.

Teeth like a branch of a spiky brush.
His tail moves like a branch on a windy day.

When he sleeps he snores so loud.
Then he wakes you up because we need to go to school.

Jade Taylor (7)
Oaklands Primary School, Welwyn

Mountains

I am so high,
I can touch the sky.

But sometimes I am small,
So I can't fall.

I am usually cold,
But I have been told
That I have got snow on my head.

I am sometimes shy,
But still I can touch the sky.

I have got lots of friends,
They are nice,
And we all fly kites.

We have gone to England, Scotland and Wales,
We have gone to New Zealand,
And Australia too.

Rhys Carter-Atkinson (10)
Oaklands Primary School, Welwyn

Katie Kangaroo

Her ears are little fins on a baby shark,
Her feet are as long as a number line.

She has teeth like buds with spiky ends,
Her back is golden toffee in a sticky wrapper.

She has a pouch as large as a globe,
A nose as squashy as an old bouncy ball.

She clicks like a switch on a painted wall,
Her tail is a branch on an old hollow tree.

When she sleeps she is as quiet as a mouse,
Then she wakes with a jump and a swish of her tail.

Oliver Mawer (7)
Oaklands Primary School, Welwyn

I Have An Oasis

I have an oasis
It's up in space
Away from the school
And my sister moaning,
Away from the small
And the tiny place
Away from the noise
And all the soft toys
Away from home
And my sister's dome
What more can I need
Than my computer friend?
The asteroid's small but it will do,
On Mars up there
On the top of the world.

George Wallis-Smith (8)
Oaklands Primary School, Welwyn

The Stream

I grow up in the mountains all dirty and cold,
Then I wash into a river now clean and making friends.

I drive away into a town still happy and clean,
Then I reach a hole and flow into a stream.

I lose my friends while getting older and older,
In a pool of horrid stinging chemicals.

Then I am sucked into a pipe nearly dead,
Then into a big bottle like a thick drowning hospital bed.

I am placed in a shop window then taken from a boy,
I am sucked into a mouth,
Then my life is at an end.

Rachael Writer-Davies (10)
Oaklands Primary School, Welwyn

I Have An Oasis

It's down on the ground
Away from the homework
And from the pain,
Away from the upset
And the cross and the SATs,
Away from my sisters
And my mum and dad,
Away from shooting
And madness and spiders,
Away from the poor
What more could I need?
I play in the park
I go on the swings
In the field
It's down on the ground.

Hannah Young (8)
Oaklands Primary School, Welwyn

Hammy The Hamster

Hammy the hamster has ears like sharp swords.
Teeth like thin squares of chocolate on yummy chocolate bars.

Her back's a big, ginger, fluffy pom-pom.
Her tail is a tiny little white stump.

She has a nose like a pink ball in the beaming sun.
When she sleeps she looks like a small ginger ball!

Then she wakes you with a nip and a pinch
And you shout.

Erin Van-Tam (7)
Oaklands Primary School, Welwyn

I Have An Oasis

I have an oasis
It's up in the trees
Away from SATs
And the shouting in the trees
Away from the RE
And the upset and spiders
Away from the madness
And maths test and insects
Away from the hairdresser
And from tests
Away from doing my hair
What more do you need?
I go to swimming
And dive like dolphins
In my big swimming pool
On the top of the world.

Emily Tomlinson (8)
Oaklands Primary School, Welwyn

Pat The Cat

Pat the cat has ears like fins.
Teeth like pieces of a sweet pine cone.

Her eyes are beautiful, a lovely green like the sapphire sky.
She has a tail like a long, thin, slithery snake.

Her nose is a soggy, old, black ball.
Her back is like a velvety shiny cushion.

When she sleeps she's as silent as an empty playground.
Then she wakes with a stretch and a tiger roll.

Sian Fuller (7)
Oaklands Primary School, Welwyn

Space

I hold everything that has ever existed safely
In my pocket
People try to find my many, many secrets
By sending up big spaceships.

I care for every living thing and let them live
In my house
But I can create creatures of dark to kill, to rip
To tear

Or I can grab all life by the throat and choke it
Till it's all dead

Sometimes I just get bored of taking care of
All pets
When I come back all my pets are dead
So I go and start afresh.

Ged Wren (10)
Oaklands Primary School, Welwyn

Amazing Animal

Fraya the fox has ears like tunnels,
And teeth like twigs with icicles on.

Her back is pieces of orange wool from a sewing box.
Her nose is a wet, black, squashy blob of play dough.

And her tail is a ponytail of a princess, all soft and cosy.
When she sleeps her mouth opens to show her shiny silver teeth.

Then she wakes and opens her large brown eyes wide.

Heather Holden (7)
Oaklands Primary School, Welwyn

Lightning

I can come when you least expect me
I could zap you on the arm, the head or the knee

If you know I'm there don't hide under a tree
Because I can still see that you are there

I can cause so much damage
I can set fire to the forest so quickly

I could kill you
By zapping your shoe

I can fly across the sky like an aeroplane
Or I could come down like a fork to a plate

I could come really fast
Or I could come really slowly

Because I am the lightning that strikes again.

Robert Vaughan (9)
Oaklands Primary School, Welwyn

The Water

I can water your flowers
Or sink your big ship.

I can whistle long ancient songs,
And make your path slippery so you slip and slide.

I can let your small dinghy float on the tide,
And make a bad hair day.

I could also get you all wet today,
But usually I'm just for play!

Ryan O'Driscoll (9)
Oaklands Primary School, Welwyn

Snow

I can be gentle,
Or I can be hard,
I can just flow,
Through your backyard.

I can go left,
Or I can right,
I can come anytime,
Including the night.

I can spin,
Or I can swirl,
I could be a boy,
Or be a girl.

I'm just like you,
I can have fun,
Not if there's a storm
But if there's a sun.

I can run,
And I can walk,
I can do anything,
Even talk.

I could stay but,
I have to go,
Remember my name,
Mr Snow.

Oliver Stephens (9)
Oaklands Primary School, Welwyn

The Clock

I have a head like a person.
I have two hands pointed anywhere I want to.
I can tell the time and change the time.
I have wires inside of me but you don't.
I am the clock.

Adam Nye (11)
Oaklands Primary School, Welwyn

I Have An Oasis

My brother came
And chased me
But I go in my cupboard

I go in my ultimate place
The magic library
Away from the screaming
And the running

So I can have peace
For reading a book
I wish, I wish I could go into a book

All of a sudden I'm
In the book
Amazing
But then the library
Is gone

And I am back in my bedroom . . .

Joshua Heyman (9)
Oaklands Primary School, Welwyn

I Have An Oasis

I have an oasis,
It's up in my Merc
Away from the tickling
And the irritating work,
Away from the extremely bad noise,
And away from my book,
Away from the sleeping
And the spider's evil looks
Away from the stress
And the snails curled
Away from the stars on top of the world.

Maxwell Brendish (8)
Oaklands Primary School, Welwyn

Snow

I am soft
But also hard.

Because I can fight the sun
I can also frighten the sun with my biggest storm yet.

Whenever I am small
I can have a great fall.

I have a big storm
To come to me now.

So have lots of fun
In the nice snow.

Brodie Collingwood (9)
Oaklands Primary School, Welwyn

The Shining Sun

I wake people in the early morning,
And sleep in my bed of clouds.

I raise a happy child's hopes,
Making everyone happy.

I strip a coat from a man,
Or brighten someone's day.

When I am happy I feel all warm,
But when I am sad or ashamed I hide behind the clouds.

I love the day and hate the night.

I am the shining sun.

Thomas Deards (10)
Oaklands Primary School, Welwyn

The Rain

I can swim through pools with just a touch,
And gather round puddles with a mighty splash.

My drops are tears when people hate me,
I can soak them and soak them till they feel regret.

Floods I can make after a while,
Deeper you'll drown then disappear.

The drops I have are sparkling silver,
I'm like see-through glass that is very fast.

When I am slow it's such a pity,
But when I am nowhere I'm a ghost with shimmering cold air.

This is what rain is like.

Louise Graham (9)
Oaklands Primary School, Welwyn

The Snow

Sliding down the wind so fast,
Landing on the grass I can.

I can dance around,
I can sit on the ground.

I can jump in the sky so high,
I can make a snowman's eye.

A cold I can catch,
I could catch a fly.

Now driving the air I have to go.

Mark Wong (9)
Oaklands Primary School, Welwyn

Water

I run a stream slowly and quietly
I pick up rocks and sticks and carry fish
At night I'm fast asleep but during the day I'm awake
I can carry your mum, dad, everyone in the world if I wanted to
I'm strong as ice when I'm frozen
I can kill someone when I'm mad or when I'm calm
I can rock you gently
When I'm around I breathe and live but when I'm not I die peacefully.

Callum France (10)
Oaklands Primary School, Welwyn

The Stream

I run down a stream, watering the flowers.
I can be low or high, but I can't touch the sky.
I can be cold or hot, I should be kind but I'm not
I can be smooth or rough.
I'm normal, though but not very soft.
I need my sleep, and all of this talking is hurting my head.

Josh Genever (10)
Oaklands Primary School, Welwyn

Earthquake

You can build buildings up but they
Won't stay long because I can make them fall down.

I can come when you least expect
So don't hide under a car because I can still see you there.

When I appear, I don't stay long
To avoid being caught.

Strike me at the heart I will not die

If you're in my way, I can shake you bone to bone.

Alexander Woods (9)
Oaklands Primary School, Welwyn

I Have An Oasis

I have an oasis
It's on top of the mountains
Away from the stress
And school
Away from my sister
And the dangers life may hold
Away from the telling off
And shouting
Life's a blast when you're on top of a mountain
Galloping with a herd of snow unicorns
With a touch of magic from their horn
I lay in their den
I see a light from above my head
And I watch the unicorns glow
I love living in the snow.

Bryony Smith (9)
Oaklands Primary School, Welwyn

My Oasis

Down in monkey world
Away from bullying
And away from school
Away from dinner
And away from dying
What else would I do for
Looking
At the monkeys in
Monkey world?

Ellis Blake (8)
Oaklands Primary School, Welwyn

I Have An Oasis

I have an oasis
It's up in my wardrobe
Away from the nagging
And my brother,
Away from tidying
And too much exhaustion,
Away from noise
And distraction,
Away from stinging nettles
And thistles,
Away from petrol stations
What more could I need?
I play with Lego
I make great models
And look in my nature book
In my bedroom.

Simon Goldsmith (9)
Oaklands Primary School, Welwyn

Rain

I can make you drenched,
or I can not let you play.

I can get you wet,
or I can get you soaked.

I can make ice,
or I can just be liquid.

I can be gentle,
or I can be strong.

Samuel Borrie (9)
Oaklands Primary School, Welwyn

I Have An Oasis

I have an oasis
It's up on an island
Away from the chocolate
And away from the spiders
Away from the junk food
And alarm clock
Away from my sister
And away from the pens and pencil
Away from the shops
And away from the madness
I will feel relaxed at my favourite place
I will jump in the ocean
And swim around
I would come out and dry
And get a fine tan.

Rhian Mather (9)
Oaklands Primary School, Welwyn

Volcanoes

I get cross
When I am hot

I scream
When I get sad

When I shoot up
It looks like I'm ill

When I die
I'm no longer alive.

Luke Fuller (9)
Oaklands Primary School, Welwyn

Sea

Cities I can smash with my big waves
Or be calm and let the children play

I can be warm on a hot summer day
Or be freezing, as cold as ice

I can be fierce and my waves rough
Or I can be kind my waves just right

I can be reckless and turn boats over
Or let people snorkel and see all my life

I have some that are big and dangerous
Or some that are small and harmless

My waves can kill people
Or sometimes save them.

Matthew Catterick (11)
Oaklands Primary School, Welwyn

My Oasis

I have an oasis
It's down under the house
Away from the questions
And the anger of the missing Lego
Away from the homework
And when I can't find toys
What more could I need?
I play with my k'nex
And cards on my secret hideout
Under the world.

Harvey Turner (8)
Oaklands Primary School, Welwyn

The Sun

I have a face that can beam,
That can make children laugh.

I can shine through your window,
And keep you warm on holiday.

I can touch your skin without you knowing,
But I have a heart of gold.

Sometimes I can get nasty,
And burn you with my entire wrath.

In the night I sleep in my bed,
Without a whisper, nothing said.

Every year I get older and older,
But eventually I will pass away.

Richard Vaughan (9)
Oaklands Primary School, Welwyn

I Have An Oasis

I have an oasis,
It's up in my room,
Away from my brother,
Away from dogs,
And away from buzzing bees,
Away from bullies,
I'll hide in my kitchen,
And in my room,
I'll go to my mum and dad,
Or in my wardrobe,
What else could I do?

Georgina Shortland (9)
Oaklands Primary School, Welwyn

The Ocean

I can whisk you away
In the night and day
I can knock you overboard
No matter what you say.

I can help you learn
How to sail a boat
But however nice you are
I may not keep you afloat.

In just a matter of time
I can destroy a house
Or I can be calm and quiet
As quiet as a mouse.

Adam Wetherall (9)
Oaklands Primary School, Welwyn

Volcanoes

I shoot out lava as fast as a fan,
It runs down my spine as slow as it can.

I destroy all the towns and burn everything,
All the bells in the town I make them go ring.

I'm the hottest thing with the biggest hole,
The people are dead because they don't have a soul.

I never was happy to erupt again,
But the problem was I had no lava to gain.

I flow like saliva and destroy all the goods,
You might not believe I burnt all the wood.

George Ironton (10)
Oaklands Primary School, Welwyn

I Have A Planet

I have a planet,
It's up in space
Away from my cousin smacking me
And away from horrible green tea,
Away from the loud noise
Away from the naughty boys,
Away from my nagging mum
And away from my uncle's amazing tum,
Away from the musical band,
What more could I want?
As I explore my wonderful world,
I feel very safe,
On my special place up in space.

Emily Beswick (9)
Oaklands Primary School, Welwyn

The Lightning

I can streak through trees and uproot the flowers,
I can fly about the sky in my black cloud car.

I can strike at any time I want,
I can scream and shout when it is befitting.

We travel in packs reeking havoc and all,
The birds when I come fall quiet in awe.

When I'm on top of life I fill with glee,
But when I'm down and low I feel lifeless and sad.

I can pound on your windows and knock on your doors
But when I strike, you will be no more.

Joel Khalili (10)
Oaklands Primary School, Welwyn

I Have An Oasis

I have an oasis
It's in our little house
Away from the shouting
It's as quiet as a mouse
People can't tell me what to do
I can mess about and act like a fool
I have all my stuff there
And my guinea pig - Patches
I'll lock the doors
And my brother can't snatch it
But I'll let young William in
Sometimes he makes me grin
I've got all sorts down there
What more do I need?

Charlotte Birtles (8)
Oaklands Primary School, Welwyn

I Have An Oasis

I have an oasis
Away from the cars
And away from my brother and dog
Away from the fighting
Away from the work
And away from the annoying fog
Away from the moon and near to the sun
And I'm always allowed to play around
My place is my gym
What more could I need
Than a quiet place with no sound?

Rhianne Batty (8)
Oaklands Primary School, Welwyn

I Have An Oasis

I have an oasis
It's up in the trees
Away from the loudness
And away from the fighting
Away from the pulling and pushing
And away from the crying
I like to be near animals
My big cats, my tigers, lions, black panthers and
Cliff cats too
Away from the shooting bananas from the monkeys
I have a code for on top of the world,
My house
Reading my book
I love my oasis.

Aimee Rayner-Okines (8)
Oaklands Primary School, Welwyn

I Have An Oasis

I have an oasis
It's away with technology
Away from the noise
And the wrath of sprouts
Away from the hedgepigs
And annoying school
Away from my brother
I kill Gargerensis
And Kronos too
On my computer.

James Curtis (8)
Oaklands Primary School, Welwyn

I Have An Oasis

I have an oasis,
It's up in the galaxy
Away from school
And my sister,
Away from the noise
And the anger,
Away from fire
And SATs
What more can I need?
I play on my PS2
And in the pool
In the middle of Jupiter.

Amanveer Benning (8)
Oaklands Primary School, Welwyn

I Have An Oasis

I have an oasis
It's up in the clouds
Away from my brother
And the shouting of the crowd,
Away from my homework
And from the yapping of the dogs,
Away from shopping
And from the rush,
What more could I need?
I have snowy mountains
And polar bears to play with,
I have an oasis,
Up in the clouds.

Lucy Reynolds (8)
Oaklands Primary School, Welwyn

I Have An Oasis

It's up in the galaxy
Away from my brother
And away from my dad.

Away little literacy, writing stories
And feeding the fish,
Away from eating fish

What more can I need?
I'll play football
I'll roast my potatoes

I'll take a swimming pool
I'll play on my PlayStation
All day long!

Harry Ironton (8)
Oaklands Primary School, Welwyn

I Have An Oasis

I have an oasis
It's on Mars
Away from my brother
And literacy handwriting,
Away from my cat
And the rush of the morning
Away from walking to school every day
What more could I need?
I eat cheese and Mars bars and
Play on the PlayStation
And do anything I want and
Play football and cricket all day.

Samuel Curtis (8)
Oaklands Primary School, Welwyn

The Calm Blue Waves

The beautiful, calm sea washing the shells onto the beach,
When the people go fishing the fishes' tails are swimming to and fro
In the deep blue sea.
The sea starts rising and the people start crying,
Swish, swish, swish, swoosh go the waves crashing and rolling onto
the shore.

Swish, swoosh, goes the waves tumbling down onto sandy shore of
the beach,
Washing shells and seaweed onto the sand littering the beach.
I love the waves because they look like prancing, dancing horses
Leaping, jumping over the clear, blue waves till the sun goes down.
I love the waves, the wonderful waves.

Georgia Conway (8)
Sherington Primary School, Charlton

The Waves

The waves crash onto the beach
Washing the shells and tiny creatures onto the sand.
The calm sea splashes gently across the shore as the
Ships zoom through the ocean sending the water
Shooting across the beach.
The little fishing boats row smoothly out to sea
As the fish swim away as fast as they can.

Thomas Dalton (8)
Sherington Primary School, Charlton

Waves

The waves are crashing in the sand
The waves are destroying the land

The waves bring golden sand
Like a golden rock band

The waves are unstoppable
But also beautiful
The waves are like an earthquake

Some big waves roll into small tiny waves
A wave is like an acrobat flying in the sun or rain
For days and days and days
The waves will never stop crashing in the land.

George Nicolaou (8)
Sherington Primary School, Charlton

The Calm Blue Sea

When the people are fishing the fish start swishing,
When the sea starts rising everyone is crying,
Even after a little while they're putting the fish in a file!

When the fish see the pointer they take the food and run away,
Some fish don't succeed, end up being shark feed,
The fish who can swim away always say you should exercise
twice a day!

Claire Linden (8)
Sherington Primary School, Charlton

Waves

Waves come crashing up and down
Breaking stones and washing rocks away.

Bringing us shells and treats
Making us wet giving us fun and joy.

Melting sandcastles
And keeping us cool.

There's a lot of things waves can do
That's why everyone loves them too.

Jacob Gleed
Sherington Primary School, Charlton

The Waves

Sitting at Antarctica

The waves are small
Going up and down
The waves are bigger than ever before.
The waves are like earthquakes
The waves are beautiful
The waves are unstoppable
Some waves roll into little waves.

Perry Hills
Sherington Primary School, Charlton